JOSÉ ORTEGA Y

HISTORY AS
A SYSTEM

and other Essays Toward
a Philosophy of History

WITH AN AFTERWORD
BY JOHN WILLIAM MILLER

The Norton Library
W · W · NORTON & COMPANY · INC ·
NEW YORK

Contents

TRANSLATOR'S FOREWORD

A TRANSLATOR should stay backstage where he belongs. If in this case he appears on the scene, it is to render thanks.

More deeply than words can express I feel indebted to Mrs. Norton, who has smoothed and shaped this translation with that careful patience and felicitous ingenuity so well known from her own work.

I acknowledge with thanks the courtesy of the Clarendon Press, Oxford, and of Professor William C. Atkinson, which made it possible to include in this volume Professor Atkinson's translation of "History as a System."

I am also obliged to Miss Eleanor Clark for permitting me to use her translation of "Unity and Diversity of Europe."

HELENE WEYL

Princeton, New Jersey
December, 1940

AUTHOR'S FOREWORD

I SHOULD have liked to present to American readers the yield of my endeavors during these last ten years; but my last ten years have not been favorable to a manuscribe's tranquil occupation. Spain's misfortunes, my own rather involuntary peregrinations, sicknesses of the kind that have us play poker singlehanded with death itself have prevented me from roofing over the two structures on which, for the first time in my life, I have been working with steadfastness and without improvisation. Meanwhile the publisher exerts on me his energetic as well as gentle influence—energetic from the determination with which he asks for a new book of mine, gentle from his own character prevailing over his energy.

The reader must therefore approach this volume with unwonted good will. Except for "History as a System," the essays it contains are either a university course ("Man the Technician"), or pages which have been written in my country's difficult times ("Unity and Diversity of Europe"), or slightly earlier material ("The Sportive Origin of the State"). This last essay, originally a lecture, is, however, a good example of what I want to say. It contains a few insights which, in view of the time when they were gained, are perhaps not undeserving of consideration.

Buenos Aires
December, 1940

1

The Sportive Origin of the State

I

SCIENTIFIC truth is characterized by its exactness and the certainty of its predictions. But these admirable qualities are contrived by science at the cost of remaining on a plane of secondary problems, leaving intact the ultimate and decisive questions. Of this renunciation it makes its essential virtue, and for it, if for nought else, it deserves praise. Yet science is but a small part of the human mind and organism. Where it stops, man does not stop. If the physicist detains, at the point where his method ends, the hand with which he delineates the facts, the human being behind each physicist prolongs the line thus begun and carries it on to its termination, as an eye beholding an arch in ruins will of itself complete the missing airy curve.

It is the task of physics to ascertain for each fact occurring here and now its principle, that is to say the preceding fact that causes it. But this principle in its turn has a principle, and so down to a first original principle. The physicist refrains from searching for first principles, and he does well. But, as I said, the man lodged in each physicist does not resign himself. Whether he likes it or not, his mind is drawn towards the last enigmatic cause of the universe. And it is natural that it should be thus. For living means dealing with the world, turning to it, acting in it, being occupied with it. That is why man is practically unable, for psychological reasons, to do without all-round knowledge of the world, without an integral idea of the universe. Crude or refined, with our consent or without it, such a trans-scientific picture of the world will settle in the mind of each of us, ruling our lives more effectively than scientific truth.

The past century, resorting to all but force, tried to restrict the human mind within the limits set to exactness. Its violent effort to turn its back on last problems is called agnosticism. But such endeavor seems neither fair nor sensible. That science is incapable of solving in its own way those fundamental questions is no sufficient reason for slighting them, as did the fox with the high-hung grapes, or for calling them myths and urging us to drop them altogether. How can we live turning a deaf ear to the last dramatic questions? Where does the world come from, and whither is it going? Which is the supreme power of the cosmos, what the essential meaning of life? We cannot breathe confined to a realm of secondary and intermediate themes. We need a comprehensive perspective, foreground and background, not a maimed scenery, a horizon stripped of the lure of infinite distances. Without the aid of the cardinal points we are liable to lose our bearings. The assurance that we have found no means of answering last questions is no valid excuse for callousness towards them. The more deeply should we feel, down to the roots of our being, their pressure and their sting. Whose hunger has ever been stilled with the knowledge that he could not eat? Insoluble though they be, these problems will never cease to loom on the vault of night, stirring us with their starry twinkle—the stars, according to Heine, are night's restless golden thoughts. North and South help to orient us despite their being not precisely cities to which one can buy a railroad ticket.

We are given no escape from last questions. In one fashion or another they are in us, whether we like it or not. Scientific truth is exact, but it is incomplete and penultimate and of necessity embedded in another ultimate, though inexact, truth which I see no objection in calling a myth. Scientific truth floats in a medium of mythology; but science taken as a whole, is it not also a myth, the admirable myth of modern Europe?

II

One of these last questions, and probably that of strongest influence on our daily destinies, is the idea we hold of life. The nineteenth century, utilitarian throughout, set up a utilitarian interpretation of the phenomenon of life which has come down to us and may still be considered as the commonplace of everyday thinking. According to it, the fundamental activity of life consists of a response to and satisfaction of imperative needs; and all manifestations of life are instances of this activity—the forms of animals as well as their movements, man's mind as well as his historical works and actions. An innate blindness seems to have closed the eyes of this epoch to all but those facts which show life as a phenomenon of utility, an adaptation. Modern biology and recent historical investigations, however, have exploded the current myth and given rise to a different idea, in which life appears with a more graceful gesture.

According to this idea, all utilitarian actions aiming at adaptation, all mere reaction to pressing needs, must be considered as secondary vital functions, while the first and original activity of life is always spontaneous, effusive, overflowing, a liberal expansion of pre-existing energies. Far from being a movement enforced by an exigency—a tropism—life is the free occurrence, the unforeseeable appetite itself. Darwin believed that species equipped with eyes have been forthcoming in a millennial evolutionary process because sight is necessary or convenient in the struggle for existence against the environment. The theory of mutation and its ally, the Mendelian theory, show with a certainty hitherto unknown in biology that precisely the opposite is true. The species with eyes appears suddenly, capriciously as it were, and it is this species which changes the environment by creating its visible aspect. The eye does not come into being because it is needed. Just the contrary; because the eye appears it can henceforth be applied as a serviceable instrument. Each species builds up its stock of useful habits by selecting among, and taking advantage of, the innumerable useless actions which a living being performs out of sheer exuberance.

We may then divide organic phenomena—animal and human—into two great classes of activity, one original, creative, vital par excellence—that is, spontaneous and disinterested; the other of utilitarian character, in which the first is put to use and mechanized. Utility does not create and invent; it simply employs and stabilizes what has been created without it.

If we leave aside organic forms and consider only the

actions of living beings, life always presents itself as an effort, but an effort of two different kinds, one made for the sheer delight of it, as Goethe says:

Das Lied, das aus der Kehle dringt,
Ist Lohn, der reichlich lohnet;

the other compulsory, an exertion in which we are urged on and worn out by a necessity imposed on us and not of our invention or desire. If the classic instance of the obligatory effort which strictly satisfies a need is to be found in what man calls work, the other, the effort *ex abundantia cordis*, becomes most manifest in sport.

We thus feel induced to invert the inveterate hierarchy. Sportive activity seems to us the foremost and creative, the most exalted, serious, and important part of life, while labor ranks second as its derivative and precipitate. Nay more, life, properly speaking, resides in the first alone; the rest is relatively mechanic and a mere functioning. To give a concrete example: the true vital phenomenon is the development of an arm and its possible movements. Once the arm with its possibilities exists, its motion in a given case is simply a mechanical matter. In the same way the eye, having come into being, sees in accordance with the laws of optics; but one cannot make an eye with optical laws. Queen Christina of Sweden remarked to Descartes, who upheld the mechanical nature of living beings, that she had never seen her watch give birth to baby watches.

This must by no means be understood as though utilitarian reaction did not in its turn inspire the sportive power, providing it with stimuli for new creations. What I want to say is that in every vital process the first impulse is given by an energy of supremely free and exuberant character, in individual life as well as in history. In the history of every living entity we shall always find that life at first is prodigal invention and that it then selects among the possibilities thus created, some of which consolidate in the form of useful habits. Merely passing in review the film of our own lives reveals our individual destinies to be the result of the selection made by actual circumstances among our personal possibilities. The individual we grow to be in the course of our lives is only one of the many we might have been but had to leave behind—lamentable casualties of our inner army. It is important to enter existence with ample possibilities in order that we may oblige destiny, the fatal pruning knife, always to leave us with some sturdy shoots intact. Abundance of possibilities is a symptom of thriving life, as utilitarianism, the attitude of confining oneself to the strictly necessary, like the sick man who begrudges every expenditure of energy, discloses weakness and waning life.

Success in life depends on amplitude of possibilities. Every blow we receive must serve as another impulse towards new attempts.

My reader will forgive me. I never conceive of this idea without its bringing back to memory the triumphant scene which the circus clowns of my childhood used to perform. A clown would stroll in with his livid, floured face, seat himself on the railing, and produce from his bulky pocket a flute which he began to play. At once the ringmaster appeared and intimated to him that here one could not play. The clown, unperturbed, stalked over to another place and started again. But now the ringmaster walked up angrily and snatched his melodious toy from him. The clown remained unshaken in face of such misfortune. He waited till the ringmaster was gone, and plunging his hand into his fathomless pocket produced another flute and from it another melody. But alas, inexorably, here came the ringmaster again, and again despoiled him of his flute. Now the clown's pocket turned into an inexhaustible magic box from which proceeded, one after another, new musical instruments of all kinds, clear and gay or sweet and melancholy. The music overruled the veto of destiny and filled the entire space, imparting to all of us with its impetuous, invincible bounty a feeling of exultation, as though a torrent of strange energies had sprung from the dauntless melody the clown blew on his flute as he sat on the railing of the circus. Later I thought of this clown of the flute as a grotesque modern form of the great god Pan of the forest whom the Greeks worshiped as the symbol of cosmic vitality—serene, goat-footed Pan who plays the sacred syrinx in the sinking dusk and with its magic sound evokes an echo in all things: leaves and fountains shiver, the stars begin to tremble, and the shaggy goats dance at the edge of the grove.

Let us say without further ado, then, that life is an affair of flutes. It is overflow that it needs most. He who rests content with barely meeting necessity as it arises will be washed away. Life has triumphed on this planet because it has, instead of clinging to necessities, deluged it with overwhelming possibilities, so that the failure of one may serve as a bridge for the victory of another.

The expression most fragrant with the scent of life, and one of the prettiest in the dictionary, is to my mind the word "incitement." It has no meaning except in the disciplines of life. Physics does not know of it. In physics one thing does not incite another; it causes it and the cause produces an effect in proportion to itself. A billiard ball colliding with another imparts to it an impulse in principle equal to its own; cause and effect are equal.

But when the spur's point ever so lightly touches its flank, the thoroughbred breaks into a gallop, generously out of proportion to the impulse of the spur. The reaction of the horse, rather than a response to an outer impulse, is a release of exuberant inner energies. Indeed, a skittish horse, with its nervous head and fiery eye, is a splendid image of stirring life. Thus we imagine the magnificent stallion whom Caligula called *Incitatus* and made a member of the Roman Senate.

Poor life, that lacks the elasticity to dart off in prancing enterprises! Sad life, that lets the hours pass in lassitude, the hours which should flash like quivering foils. A melancholy fate for a Spaniard to live in an epoch of Spanish indolence and to remember the charger's rearing and the tiger-leaps of which in better times Spain's history consisted. Where has her vigor gone? Does it await resurrection in her hoary soil? I want to believe it; and resigned to feed on images, since nothing else is left to me, I draw comfort from this:

Córdoba is one of those cities whose soil is saturated with historical memories. Under the present quiet and humble town sleeps what remains of six civilizations: Roman, Gothic, Arabic, Hebrew, Spanish of the classic and of the romantic periods. Each of them may be epitomized in one august name: Seneca, Alvaro, Averroes, Maimonides, Góngora, Duque de Rivas. And all these treasures of creative power lie buried under the drowsy surface. Córdoba is a rosebush with its roots in the air and its roses underground.

Now it happened a few years ago that as workmen were digging in the patio of a palace belonging to a lady of ancient descent, on Claudio Marcelo Street, their spades struck against a hard object. They looked closer and saw something like the ear of a bronze horse. They dug on, and there emerged before their wondering eyes the splendid head of a horse and then the beginning of an equestrian statue of Roman style—perhaps the statue of Claudius Marcellus himself. They apprised the lady, she informed herself of the possible cost of the excavation and, finding it prohibitive, ordered the statue to be covered with earth again. And there he remained in his tomb, incredible though it seems, the Spanish *Incitatus* with his fine strong neck and his sensitive, foam-flecked mouth. But as the Breton fishermen, when leaning over the sides of their boats on calm afternoons, believe that they hear bells ringing from the bottom of the sea, thus one might fancy that if one held one's ear to the ground one would hear the desperate subterranean neighing of that great bronze horse.

But we have to continue our way.

III

Youth!—In some not too distant future I hope to quarry the rich vein of secrets we come upon in psychology of youth. In general, the time is ripe for a resolute attack on the great biological themes of childhood, youth, maturity, senility.

I beg leave to prophesy for the near future a converging of scientific attention on the problem of ages common to all organisms, not only plants, animals, and human beings. Before long, one of the great themes of thought will be the tragic fact of the aging of races. Then will biology become aware of the necessity of starting the analysis of the secret of life from the obvious, though unheeded, fact of the inevitability of death.

Here we are concerned only with a feature peculiar to the psychology of youth.

In attempting to distinguish different phases in the mental development of a child, one would have to look for an inner activity free from influences of the will and the environment and would have to study the changes this activity has undergone year by year. Dreams, for example. Analysis of dreams suggests a division into three periods. First the child dreams that he plays alone. At the second stage a new personage enters the scene, another child, but this child plays only the role of a spectator; it is present to watch the dreamer play. Then comes a third and last period, close to puberty, when the child's dreams are invaded by a whole group of boys who play with him, and into whose turbulent band his individual person merges.

Indeed, one of the forces decisive in the adolescent soul, and one which still gains strength in that of the full-grown youth, is the desire to live together with other boys of the same age. The isolation of infancy breaks down, and the boy's personality flows out into the coeval group. He no longer lives by himself and for himself; he no longer feels and wishes as an individual; he is absorbed by the anonymous personality of the group which feels and wishes for him. That is why youth is the season of friendship. Boys and young men, still unformed as individuals, live submerged in the group of the young which drifts undivided and inseparable over the fields of life wherever the wind may carry it. I call this urge to sociability the instinct of coevality.

One day a boy of twelve, sensitive and limpid of soul, who is near to my heart, came to his mother and said: "Mamma, tomorrow we are all going on an excursion with the school, boys and girls. I want my suit to be pressed. You must give me a silk handkerchief and five pesetas for candies." Knowing her son as a rough-and-ready young man, the mother, surprised at so much ur-

banity, asked what it was all about. And the boy candidly
replied: "You know, Mamma, we have begun to like the
girls." Now, he himself did not yet like the girls. What
had happened was that the group of schoolboys as such
had felt the first stir of the curiosity of sex, a vague
presentiment of the charm of femininity and the dynamic
grace of the struggle between the man's gallant wooing
and the coyness of the woman. The first impulse of puberty had appeared in the group before it had appeared
in the individual, and the lively band, glowing with solidarity like a football team, had decided to join battle
against the eternal feminine. Needless to say, when on
that famous day their valiant troop came up against the
pertness of the maidens, they were dumbfounded, and
could not even muster enough courage to brandish the
sweet bribe of candies.

Human history seems to proceed with a double
rhythm: the rhythm of age and the rhythm of sex. In
some epochs the youthful influence prevails; others are
ruled by mature men. At any rate, directly after the
formless form of human society which sociologists call
the horde, we find a society endowed with a beginning of
organization, the principle of which is that of age. The
social body has grown in numbers, and from a horde it
has developed into a tribe. Primitive tribes are divided
into three social classes which are not economic, as so-

cialistic dogma would have it, but are the groups of youth, maturity, and old age. No other distinctions have yet developed. The family, in particular, is still unknown; so much so, in fact, that all members of the class of the young call themselves brothers, naming all those of the older class father. The first social organization divides the tribe not into families, but into so-called age-classes.

Among these three ages, however, the one that predominates through power and authority is not the class of the mature men, but that of the youths. In fact, this is frequently the only class, and a number of facts, which it is unnecessary to detail here, show beyond doubt that it is the first to be organized. What has happened in the transition from the shapeless horde to the organized tribe?

The hordes had been roaming for years without coming upon each other. The number of individuals of the human species on the whole planet was still exceedingly small. But there must have befallen an unusually prolific epoch which densified the population enough to bring the hordes closer together. This increase in population is a symptom of higher vitality in the species, and of growing perfection of its faculties.

Now it comes to pass that the boys of two or three neighboring hordes, driven by the desire for coeval comradeship, decide to unite and to live together—obviously not for the purpose of remaining idle. Youth is sociable, and at the same time eager for hazardous enterprises. Infallibly, one of a temperament more imaginative or bold or deft than the rest will rise among them and propose the great venture. They all feel, without knowing why, a strange and mysterious disgust for the familiar women of their own blood with whom they live in the horde and an appetite sharpened by imagination for the others, those alien women, unknown, unseen, or only fleetingly espied.

And now one of the most prodigious events of human history takes place, an event from which gigantic consequences have sprung. They decide to rape girls of distant hordes. But that is no gentle enterprise. A horde does not meekly tolerate the abduction of its women. To rob them one has to fight; and war is born for the service of love. War calls for a leader and necessitates discipline, thus bringing into being authority, law, and social structure. But unity of leadership and discipline entails and fosters unity of spirit, a common concern in the great problems of life. And we find, as a matter of fact, that the ceremonies and rituals of the cult of magic powers originate in these associations of youths.

Life in common begets the idea of building a permanent and spacious dwelling, an abode different from the occasional den and the simple shelter against the wind. The first house built by man is not a home for the family, still nonexistent, but a casino for young men. Here they prepare for their expeditions and perform their rituals; here they indulge in chanting, drinking, and wild banquets. Whether we approve of it or not, the club is older than the family, the casino older than the domestic hearth.

Mature men, women, and children are prohibited on pain of death from entering the casino of the young, which ethnologists, because of its later forms, call the bachelor house. It is all mystery, secret, taboo. For, surprisingly enough, these primitive associations of youths took on the character of secret societies with iron discipline, in which the members through severe training developed proficiency in war and hunting. That is to say, the primeval political association is the secret society; and while it serves the pleasures of feasting and drinking, it is at the same time the place where the first religious and athletic asceticism is practiced. We must not forget that the literal translation of the word "asceticism" is "training exercise." The monks took it over from the sport vocabulary of the Greek athletes. *Ascesis* was the regime of the life of an athlete, and it was crammed with exercises and privations. Thus we may well say that the club of the young is not only the first house and the first casino, but also the first barrack and the first monastery.

The deities, as I have said, are the gods of the hunter, the animals; and their cult is of orgiastic and magic character. Man wins the good will of the sacred animal powers by imitating animal forms and movements. On the solemn days of the god's great festivals the youthful band cover their faces with horrid masks and animal heads and dance through the fields in wild ecstasy. They hurl a piece of wood into the air which, swinging at the end of a cord, produces a weird noise at the sound of which women and children scatter, for they are forbidden to see the fantastic troop of dancers as it departs in drunken rapture for a raid on alien women. The mask that is worn at festivals is also the costume of war. Festivals, hunts, and wars long remained indistinguishable. That is why almost all primitive dances are stylized hunting or warlike gestures.

All these remarks which space here compels me to set down in a somewhat breathless manner are no mere hypotheses of my own. Every act we have described may, in its essentials, be occurring somewhere on the earth in this moment.

We have seen, then, that the first human society is precisely the opposite of a reaction to imposed necessities. It is an association of the young for the purpose of raping the women of alien tribes and performing all sorts of barbarous exploits. Rather than a parliament or a cabinet of bigwigs, it resembles an athletic club.

What in refined epochs of decadence and romanticism was to become the dream of the *princesse lointaine* in rough and primitive times gave rise, as we have seen, to the first organization of society. It brought about exogamy, that is to say, the primary nuptial law which commands the seeking of a wife outside the circle of blood relations. The biological importance this has had for the human species need hardly be stressed. The first matrimony was robbery, rape—of which symbolical traces remain in many later wedding ceremonies and even in the vocabulary of love itself, since the impetuous desire of love is called rapture.

IV

We have found that the clubs of the young introduced into history the following phenomena: exogamy, war, authoritative organization, training or asceticism, the law, cultic associations, the festival of masked dances or carnival, and the secret society. And all this indistinguishably merged into one phenomenon provides the irrational historical origin of the state. Again we see that in the beginning there is vigor and not utility.

There can be small doubt, however, that this epoch of

unrestricted and uncontrolled predominance of tempes-
tuous youth was a hard and cruel time. The rest of the
social mass must find some defense against the martial
and political associations of the young. They find it in
the association of the old—the senate. The mature men
live with the women and children of whom they are not,
or do not know they are, the husbands and the fathers. The
woman seeks the protection of her brothers and her
mother's brothers. She becomes the center of a social
group contrasting with the club of the young males. Here
we come upon the first family, the matriarchal family,
which, as a matter of fact, is of defensive and reactive
origin and opposed to the state. Henceforth, the principles of equal age and equal blood will strive against each
other in history. When one rises the other sinks, and vice
versa.

In this brief outline I have sought to use the origin of
the state as an instance of the creative power inherent in
the activity of sport. It was not the worker, the intellectual, the priest, properly speaking, or the businessman
who started the great political process, but youth, pre-
occupied with women and resolved to fight—the lover,
the warrior, the athlete.

I wish I might now discuss this erotic impetus, which
revealed itself as so creative a power in history. We may
find love to be the prototype of primary vitality and a

major instance of sport in the biological sphere. But it would make this essay endless, and I must still draw my reader's attention to epochs less primitive and better known to him than this hour of twilight and dawn.

Indeed, we must not fail to take advantage of the insight gained in the ethnological sphere to elucidate a few of the recalcitrant problems of full-fledged historical times. Wherever we find the truly original genesis of a political organism, whenever we catch a glimpse of the birth of a state, we infallibly come upon the youth clubs which dance and fight.

Classical historians do not know what to make of the deepest and most archaic layer we encounter in the institutions of Rome and of the Hellenic cities. In Greece these institutions are called *phyle, phratria, hetairia.* Greek scholars understand the meaning of the words but, up to now, they have not known the actuality behind it. *Phyle* means tribe but in the sense of an organized body of warriors, not of a group of blood relations. *Phratria* means brotherhood, and *hetairia* company. Before the appearance of the *polis*—the city with its constitution— these forms constituted the political structure of the Greek people. The *phratria* or brotherhood, which corresponds to the *sabha* of the Asiatic Aryans, is nothing else than the age-class of the young organized for feasts and war. We must bear in mind that, as I said before, in primitive times all youths call each other brother and call father all members of the class of those more advanced in age. *Hetairia,* or company, clearly reveals in its name the associative principle of the secret society which unites young men around a chief. It is the same as the Germanic *Gefolgschaft,* the sodality of loyal followers of one leader. In modern military parlance this original meaning is still preserved in the word "company."

The people of Attica suffered from too much intelligence. Acuity of mind is a sublime restlessness, almost an exalted form of neurasthenia, which easily disintegrates an organism. Consequently, in Athens all traditions were soon done away with and the social body embarked at once upon an era of utopian reforms which eventually destroyed it. That is why Attica preserved but scanty remains of its primitive organization.

Sparta, on the other hand, thought less and lived more robustly. Here the *phratriae,* in the form of military organizations, remain in full vigor. The warriors live together, and apart from their families. The solidarity of their companionship in war and worship is symbolized in the famous suppers at which they ate the black soup, a ritual dish. No wonder that Sparta is the scene of the rape of Helen, who first was a lunar goddess and later became an alien woman. A comparison of the facts we know about military life in Lacedaemonia with the cus-

toms of any youthful associations in contemporary so-
called savage tribes—the Masai of East Africa, for instance—will reveal a surprising resemblance between the
two.

If the state, as cannot be denied, since history proves
it repeatedly, is disintegrated by an excess of intellectual
acuity and restlessness, it, conversely, reaches its highest
degree of stability and permanence in a moderately in-
telligent nation which possesses a definite talent, the
strange innate talent of ruling. Such was the case of
Rome, as today it is that of England. And, notable resemblance, both nations are characterized by their ma-
niacal conservatism.

This explains why Rome, though it appeared on the
historical scene much later than Greece, preserves more
institutions of archaic character. Thanks to this fact, we
are able to discern under the political structure of historical Rome very old relics of its primitive institutions,
relics so old, in fact, that even the oldest Roman ar-
chaeologists failed to understand them. These institutions
were infallibly preserved as religious ceremonies, not
because they had been exclusively and properly speaking
religious, but because every archaic institution that has
lost its actual relevance tends to survive in this form.
Everything ancient that is no longer understood seems to
acquire an electric charge of mysticism that transforms

it into a religious phenomenon. The oldest division of the Roman State was into *curiae;* but by the time we see Rome in the full light of history the *curiae* are mere associations of patriotic piety charged with the cult of the tutelary deities of the city. Nobody, not even the Romans themselves, knew the origin of the word *curia.* Contemporary philologists have broken their heads trying to derive it from *cures et quirites*—the lancers—but have not succeeded in confirming this origin. We shall now see that a perfectly plausible new etymology receives unexpected corroboration from our theory of the origin of the state.

Besides the *curiae,* the most time-honored Roman institutions are the colleges and fraternities, or guilds, of priests. I will refrain from speaking of the councils of *pontifices* and *augures,* much though they pertain to our thesis, and confine myself to one society only, the archaism of whose ceremonials, costumes, rituals, and chants aroused even in the Roman of the second century B. C. a mixed feeling of respect and amusement. I mean the corporation of priests called the *Salii.* Organized, like almost all primitive Roman institutions, on the principle of duality, it consisted of two bodies of twelve members each. It was consecrated to the cult of Mars, the Latin god who stands at once for war, agriculture, and shepherding. At certain times, particularly in March, the

month of Mars, the *Salii* held their processions in which
they performed a primitive, warlike dance. Hence their
name: *Salii*, from *salire*, to leap or dance. The chief of
each of the two sections, who danced in front of the
others like the leader of a chorus, was called the *praesul*, fore-dancer, the root *sul* being the same as the *sal*
of *salire*. We may mention in this context the etymology
of *ex-sul*, the exiled, he who has leapt out over the fron-
tier, and of *in-sul-a*, island, the rock which has jumped
into the sea.[1]

The *Salii* wore a costume which looked grotesque to
the eyes of Republican Romans, but which was nothing
but an ancient war outfit, the accouterments used by the
patricians until the seventh century B. C. They carried
large shields of obsolete form which were objects of
worship in Rome precisely because the memory of their
origin had been lost. These shields were kept in a man-
sion called *curia Saliorum*. Cicero mentions that once,
when the house of the *Salii* was on fire, people found in
it the royal baton of Romulus. Which hints that there
was a connection between the guild of the *Salii* and the
foundation of the Roman State. Their chant, or *carmen
saliare*, was a hymn to Mars, who was invoked under
names and in a vocabulary so antiquated that nobody in
Rome understood them. In their *curia* the *Salii* cele-

[1] According to Mommsen, *Römische Geschichte*, vol. 1.

brated, at the cost of the state, ritual meals of such opulence that the *coena Saliorum* became proverbial in Rome.

This guild of warlike dancers manifestly shows all the features we have pointed out in the primitive youth clubs, and we find it connected with the founding of the Roman State. The processions of the *Salii* were the main attraction in a great urban festival of the same orgiastic type as the *lupercales,* which, incidentally, are one of the roots of our carnival. The *lupercal* was the festival of the *lupa* or she-wolf, the totem animal of the city of Rome. In it some citizens appeared dressed in wolf furs and were pursued by others disguised as shepherds, and all brandished thistles with which they teased the passers-by. Such a festival of herdsmen hunting the enemy wolf is celebrated in similar form by the youth associations of many African and Melanesian tribes.

But the important point is that when the Romans dethroned their kings, who as Etruscans were alien rulers, and, returning to their primitive institutions, organized their commonwealth as a republic, we see suddenly appear at the head of it, as highest officials and supreme representatives of the state, two *consules*. What are these consuls? From where does their function or even their name spring? The grammarians are still at odds about the etymology of the word; but there is one theory, maintained by Mommsen among others, which relates the word *consul* to *praesul, exsul,* and *insula.* It fits in like the keystone that finishes the arch of the political origin of Rome. For, according to it, *con-sules* are those who dance together, namely the two *praesules* or chiefs of the young warriors and dancers who were united in the associations of male youths. Their house and communion was called *curia.* Now, the most recent explanation of this expression is *curia = co-vir-ia,* that is to say, union of young men. In the form of the decadent guild of the *Salii* we evidently come upon the relics of the youthful brotherhoods, the founding brothers of the Roman State. As the crowning touch of these suggestive coincidences let us remember that the founding of the city is interwoven with the tale of the rape of the Sabine women, one of the first exploits accomplished by Romulus and his comrades. Our interpretation permits us to recognize in this legend a general and notorious fact characteristic for a certain stage of social evolution. Roman nuptial rites preserve a trace of the original rape in the well-known custom of the groom not allowing the bride to enter his house on her own feet, but carrying her over the threshold, thus demonstrating that, symbolically, she was being raped.

But the subject is inexhaustible. Let us conclude at this point our outline of the sportive origin of the state.[2]

[2] For those who are interested in such questions I will add in brief terms an equation which suggests the same origin of the state among Germanic tribes. The props of the Germanic State are the *Recken*, that is to say, the young stalwarts like Siegfried and in general the nobles of the epics. *Recke* is the same word as rich; his power is the *Reich*, and the realm reached by his power the *Reichland*. *Rike*, rich, we see, does not mean being possessed of property. The *Recke* was not "rich" because he owned the instruments of production; on the contrary, he disposed of wealth because he was *rike*: valiant, warlike.

2

Unity and Diversity of Europe

I

THERE is a story—I don't vouch for its truth—that at the time of the jubilee for Victor Hugo a reception was given at the Elysée Palace, to which representatives of all nations came to pay homage. The great poet stood in the ballroom in the solemn pose of a statue, his elbow resting on a mantel, while one by one the representatives came out from the crowd and paid him their homage, an usher announcing them in stentorian tones: "Monsieur the representative of England!" Victor Hugo, his voice quivering with emotion, eyes lifted to the ceiling, replied: "England! Ah, Shakespeare!" The usher went on: "Monsieur the representative of Spain!" And Victor Hugo: "Spain! Ah, Cervantes!" The usher: "Monsieur the representative of Germany!" Victor Hugo: "Germany! Ah, Goethe!" But next in line was a potbellied little bumpkin of a man whom the usher announced as "Monsieur the representative of Mesopotamia!" Victor Hugo, who until then had remained imperturbable and sure of himself, seemed to hesitate. His eyes circled in a wide, anxious glance as if he were searching the entire cosmos for something that eluded him, but in a moment he seemed to have found it and to feel himself once more master of the situation. And indeed in the same moving tones, with no whit less conviction, he replied to the homage of the dumpy representative: "Mesopotamia! Ah, mankind!"

I have told this anecdote by way of declaring, without Victor Hugo's solemnity, that I have never written for Mesopotamia nor addressed myself to mankind. This habit of speaking to mankind at large, the most sublime and at the same time the most contemptible form of demagogy, was adopted around 1750 by certain wayward intellectuals, ignorant of their own limitations. Though by profession men of speech, of "logos," they used it with neither care nor respect and without realizing that the word is a sacrament demanding the most delicate administration.

I am persuaded that speech, like almost everything that man does, is far more illusory than is commonly supposed. We define language as the means of revealing our thoughts. But any definition—this one included—if not indeed misleading, is ironic; it implies tacit reservations, and if not so interpreted may be exceedingly harmful. It is not so much that language serves also to hide our thoughts, to lie; lying would be impossible if original and normal speech were not sincere. Like counterfeit coin, which is carried in circulation by real money, lying is in the last analysis nothing but the humble parasite of truth.

No, the real danger lies not in the definition itself, but in the optimism with which we fill it out. For if it does not go so far as to say that language will reveal all our thought with some degree of accuracy, neither does it tell the strict truth: that it is impossible for men truly to understand one another, that they are condemned to profound loneliness and waste themselves in efforts to reach their fellow beings. Of these efforts it is language that at times comes nearest to expressing a little of what goes on within us: nothing more. As a rule, however, we make no such reservations, but engage in conversation with the express purpose of saying all we think. And in this lies the illusion. For though language may convey, more or less, some portion of our thought, it raises an insurmountable barrier against the rest. It does well enough for the statements and arguments of mathematics; when it comes to physics it is already ambiguous and inadequate; and as conversation approaches subjects more im-

portant than these, more human, more "real," it in-
creases in imprecision, crudeness, and obscurity. The
idea that by means of speech we can arrive at understanding is an age-old misconception, and it makes us
talk and listen in such good faith that often we understand far less than if we kept silent and attempted simply
to guess one another's thought.

It is too often forgotten that every authentic saying
not only says something, but is said by someone to someone. There are always a speaker and a receiver, who are
not indifferent to the meanings of words, and as they
vary so do the latter. *Duo si idem dicunt non est idem.*
All terms of speech depend on the occasion.[1] For this
reason language is essentially dialogue and is more effective in this form than in any other. I believe, therefore, that the measure of a book is the author's ability to
imagine his reader concretely and to carry on a kind of
hidden dialogue with him, in which the reader perceives
from between the lines the touch as of an ectoplasmic
hand that feels him, caresses him, or deals him an occasional gentlemanly blow.

It is because the word has been abused that it has
fallen into disrepute. As with so many other things, the
abuse has consisted in using the instrument rashly, with-

[1] *Vide* p. 205.

out awareness of its limitations. For almost two centuries it has been the general belief that to talk meant to talk *urbi et orbi*, that is, to everyone and no one. As for me, I despise this kind of communication and suffer in not knowing concretely to whom I speak.

II

This thesis, granting to the word so small a radius of action, might seem contradicted by the very fact that my own books have found readers in almost every language in Europe. I believe, however, that this is rather symptomatic of something else, something very serious, that is the frightful homogeneity of situation towards which the entire Western world is sinking. During the last ten years, this sameness has increased to an agonizing extent. I say agonizing because, actually, what is felt as painful in any one country becomes infinitely depressing when its victim discovers that there is hardly a place left in the continent where exactly the same thing is not happening. Formerly it was possible to clear the stuffy atmosphere of one country by opening its windows on to another, but this expedient no longer holds, since the air in the next country is as stifling as in our own. Hence a feeling of asphyxiation. Job, who was a terrible *pince sans rire*, asked his friends, travelers and merchants who had been around in the world: *Unde sapientia venit and quis est locus intelligentiae?*—"Do you know of any place in the world where there is intelligence?"

However, in this progressive assimilation of conditions we must distinguish two different elements, of opposing value.

This swarm of Western peoples, that set out on its flight through history from the ruins of the ancient world, has always been characterized by a dual form of life. It so happened that while each one was in the process of forming its own particular genius, among them or above them all there was being created a common fund of ideas, manners, and enthusiasms. There is, moreover, a crowning paradox in this destiny that was increasing at the same time their homogeneity and their differences, for in this case the two were not alien. On the contrary, every new unifying principle served to fertilize their diversity. The idea of Christianity engendered the national churches; the memory of the Roman *imperium* inspired the various forms of the state; the renaissance of letters in the fifteenth century let loose divergent literatures; science and the unitarian concept of man as "pure reason" created the different intellectual styles which were to lend their mold even to the farthest abstractions of mathematics. And as a culminating point, even the extravagant eighteenth-century idea of prescribing an

identical constitution for all peoples resulted in the romantic awakening of the differential consciousness of the
nationalities, and thus served to push each towards its
particular vocation.

The point is that for these so-called European peoples
to live has always meant—of course, since the eleventh
century, or since Otto III—to move and act in a common
space or environment. That is, for each one to live was
"to live with" the rest. This "living with," or coexistence,
might assume either a peaceful or a warlike form. Inter-
European wars have almost always been marked by a
curious style that gives them a certain resemblance to
family squabbles. They avoid the annihilation of the
enemy and seem rather competitions, as between two
high school teams, or the disputes of heirs over a family
legacy. In their various ways all tend towards the same
end. *Eadem sed aliter*. As Charles V said of Francis I:
"My cousin and I are in complete agreement: we both
want Milan."

It is of minor importance that to this common historic
space that all Western people consider their home there
should correspond a physical space that geography calls
Europe. The historic space that I refer to is measured by
its radius of effective and lasting coexistence—it is a
social space. Now coexistence and society are equivalent
terms. Society is that which is produced automatically

by the simple fact of coexistence. By itself, inevitably, it secretes customs, habits, language, law, and public power. One of the worst errors of "modern" thought, leaving its stain on us even today, has been to confuse society with association, which is just about its opposite. A society is not brought about by a willed agreement. Inversely, any such agreement presupposes the existence of a society, of people living together under certain customs, and the agreement can only determine one form or another of this coexistence, of this pre-existing society. The idea of society as a contractual, and therefore juridical, union is one of the silliest attempts that has ever been made to put the cart before the horse. For law, law the reality—not the idea of law in the minds of philosophers, jurists, or demagogues—is nothing, to use a rather baroque phrase, but the spontaneous secretion of society; it can be nothing else. To expect law to govern the relations between beings not already living in effective society seems to me—if I may be pardoned for my rudeness—to have a somewhat confused and ridiculous idea of law.

It is not surprising, however, that this confused and ridiculous idea of law should be widespread. One of the greatest misfortunes of our time is that the peoples of the West, coming up against the terrible public conflicts of today, have found themselves equipped with a wholly archaic set of notions on the meaning of society, collectivity, the individual, customs, law, justice, revolution, etc. A good part of the disorder of the present is due to the disproportion between the perfection of our ideas on physical phenomena and the scandalous backwardness of the "moral sciences." Most of our statesmen, professors, distinguished physicists, and novelists have opinions on these subjects worthy of a small-town barber. Is it not then quite natural that it should be the small-town barber who sets the tone of the time? [2] But to return to our subject: I wanted to suggest that for a long time the peoples of Europe have actually made up a society, a collectivity, taking these words in the same sense as when applied to the nations separately. This society has all the attributes of any: there are European manners, European customs, European public opinion, European law, and European public power. But all these social phenomena appear in a form appropriate to the stage of evolution reached by European society as a whole, which is obviously less advanced than that of its component parts, the nations.

[2] It is only fair to say that in France, and in France alone, some clarification and *mise au point* of these ideas has been attempted. The reader will find elsewhere some remarks on this attempt as well as on the reason for its failure. I, too, have tried to collaborate in this effort of clarification, starting from the recent French tradition, which is unsurpassed in this field of ideas. The result of my reflections will appear in a book to be published in the near future, *Man and People*, which will contain the development and justification of my present remarks.

For example, that form of social pressure which is public power functions in all societies, including primitive ones where there exists no special organ to handle it. If one wants to give the name of "state" to that differentiated organ charged with the exercise of public power, one may say that in certain societies there is no state, but not that there is no public power. Where there exists public opinion, how could there not be public power, if the latter is simply collective violence let loose by opinion? Now it would be hard to deny that for centuries, and with ever-greater intensity, there has been a European public opinion and even a technique of influence over it.

I therefore suggest that the reader spare the malice of a smile when I predict—somewhat boldly, in view of present appearances—a possible, a probable unification of the states of Europe. I do not deny that the United States of Europe is one of the poorest fantasies that has ever existed and I take no responsibility for what others have handed out under these verbal signs. But I do maintain that it is highly improbable that a society, a collectivity as ripe as that now formed by the peoples of Europe, should not move towards the creation of a state apparatus for the exercise of the European public power which already exists. It is not, then, a weakness for fantasy nor a leaning towards "idealism," which I despise and have fought all my life, that has brought me to this conclusion. It is historic realism that has made it clear to me that the unity of Europe as society is not an "ideal" but a very ancient daily fact, and having seen this fact one cannot but confront the probability of a general European state. As for the occasion that will suddenly bring the process to a close, it might be almost anything: a Chinaman's pigtail appearing behind the Urals or a shock from the great Islamic *magma*.

The shape of this supernational state will, of course, be very different from those to which we are accustomed, just as the national state differed from the city-state of ancient times. All that I have attempted in these pages is to free the mind of the reader so that it may keep faith with the subtle conception of society and state proposed by the European tradition.

It was never easy for Greco-Roman thought to conceive of reality as dynamic. It was not able to detach itself from the visible, or from its substitutes, as a child really understands in a book only the illustrations. All the endeavors of its philosophers to transcend this limitation were in vain. In all their efforts to understand, there functions, to a greater or less extent, as a paradigm, the corporal object which was for them the essential "thing." They could conceive only of *a* society, *a* state, whose unity was in the form of visual contiguity—for example, a city. The mental vocation of Europe is the opposite. To the European mind everything visible seems, as such, simply the apparent mask of a hidden force which is constantly producing it and is its true reality. Where the force, the *dynamis*, acts uniformly, there real unity exists, though to the eye it may give the appearance of dispersion.

We should be falling back into the limitation of the ancients were we to perceive public power only where it has assumed the well-known and, so to speak, fixed masks of state, that is, in the particular nations of Europe. In my opinion it is quite untrue that the decisive public power at work in any one of them consists exclusively of its inner or national public power. It must be realized once and for all that for centuries—and consciously during the last four—the peoples of Europe have lived under a public power so purely dynamic that it can be characterized only by names drawn from mechanical science: "European balance," or "balance of power."

This is the real government of Europe, ruling in its flight through history the swarm of peoples, industrious and belligerent as bees, that rose out of the ruins of the ancient world. The unity of Europe is not a fantasy, but reality itself; what *is* fantastic is the belief in France, Germany, Italy, or Spain as substantive and independent units. It is understandable, however, that everyone should not clearly perceive the reality of Europe, for Europe is not a "thing" but a balance. Already in the eighteenth century the historian Robertson called the balance of Europe "the great secret of modern politics." It is indeed a great and paradoxical secret! For the balance of power depends at bottom on the existence of a plurality. If the plurality is lost, the dynamic unity fades away. Europe may well be called a swarm: many bees and a single flight.

This unitary character of the magnificent European plurality is what I should call the good kind of homogeneity, fruitful and desirable, the quality that inspired Montesquieu's remark that "Europe is only a nation made up of several" [3] and moved Balzac, more romantically, to speak of "the great continental family whose efforts reach toward I know not what mystery of civilization." [4]

III

This abundance of European modes, surging constantly out of their deep-rooted unity and returning again to preserve it, is the greatest treasure of the West. The dull-witted can never grasp a concept so acrobatic, in which one jumps endlessly back and forth between

[3] *Monarchie Universelle: Deux opuscules*, 1891, p. 36.
[4] *Œuvres Complètes* (Calmann-Lévy), vol. 22, p. 248.

the affirmation of plurality and the recognition of unity.
They are sluggish spirits, born to live beneath the perpetual tyrannies of the Orient.

Today this treasure threatens to be devoured by a
form of homogeneity that has triumphed over the entire
continent. Everywhere there has arisen the mass-man,
a type of man built hurriedly, mounted on a few poor
abstractions and who is therefore identical from one
end of Europe to the other. To him is due the look
of stifling monotony that life has begun to assume
throughout the continent. He is a man emptied of his
own history, with no inward past, and so given over to
any so-called "international" discipline. He is less a
man than the shell of one, made of plain *idola fori:* he
has no insides, no inalienable privacy of his own, no
irrevocable "I." Consequently, he is always ready to
play at being anything. He has only appetites, he believes that he has only rights and no obligations; he is
a man without the imperative of nobility—*sine nobilitate*—the snob.[5]

This universal snobbism, so apparent, for example, in
the worker of the present time, has blinded men to the
fact that, if indeed all the given structure of continental
life is to be transcended, the change must be brought

---

[5] The lists of the students at Cambridge indicated beside a person's name
his profession and rank. Beside the names of commoners there appeared
the abbreviation "s.nob.": *sine nobilitate;* whence the word "snob."

about without a serious loss of its inner plurality. The snob, having been emptied of his own destiny and since it does not occur to him that he is alive for some specific and unexchangeable purpose, cannot understand that life offers particular callings and vocations. He is therefore hostile to liberalism, with the hostility of a deaf man for words. Liberty has always been understood in Europe as the freedom to be our real selves. It is not surprising that a man should want to be rid of it who knows that he has no real mission to fulfill.

With curious facility everyone has banded together to fight and denounce the old school of liberalism. It is a suspicious phenomenon, for as a rule people do not agree so easily except in matters that are somewhat underhand or foolish. I do not maintain, of course, that the idea of the old liberalism is wholly reasonable—how could it be, since it is both old and an *ism?*—but I do consider it a theory of society far clearer and more profound than is imagined by its collectivist underminers, who in the first place know very little about it. It embraces, too, a highly acute intuition of the real stuff of Europe's past.

For example, when Guizot contrasts European civilization to all others with the observation that in Europe no principle, idea, group, or class has ever triumphed in an absolute form and that to this is due its progressive character and constant growth, we cannot but take heed.[6] He knows what he is talking about; the expression of his thought is negative and therefore inadequate, but the words are charged with insight. As one knows the diver by the smell of the ocean still clinging to him, so do we recognize in Guizot a man who has plunged into the depths of European history. Indeed, it seems incredible that at the beginning of the nineteenth century, a time of rhetoric and confusion, there should have been written such a book as *The History of European Civilization.* Even a man of today can learn from it how liberty and plurality are reciprocal and between them constitute the permanent heart of Europe.

But Guizot, like the Doctrinaires in general, was never well received. This seems to me quite natural. Whenever I see a man or group attracting facile and prolonged applause I have a strong suspicion that there is something basically impure in the man or the group, however gifted they may be. I may be wrong, but if so the error is not

[6] "La coexistence et le combat de principes diverses."—*L'histoire de la civilisation en Europe,* p. 35. In a man as different from Guizot as Ranke we find the same idea: "In Europe, as soon as any principle whatsoever attempts absolute domination, it comes up against a resistance put forth by the very mainsprings of life." (*Saemtliche Werke,* vol. 38, p. 140.) And again (vol. 10, p. 3): "The European world is made up of elements of different origins, and it is precisely in their opposition and struggle that the changes of historical periods are developed." The influence of Guizot is obvious in this quotation from Ranke. One of the factors that prevents a clear understanding of certain profound levels of nineteenth-century history is that no adequate study has been made of the interchange of ideas between France and Germany, say from 1790 to 1830. Such a study might well reveal that Germany received much more from France during that period than vice versa.

willful but rather one that has been planted in me by experience. In any case I want to have the courage to assert
that this group of Doctrinaires, laughed at by everyone,
butt of the most slanderous jokes, was in my opinion the
most valuable political element on the continent in the
nineteenth century. They alone had a clear perception of
what had to be done in Europe after the Great Revolution, and moreover in their personal lives they stood for
something dignified and removed, in the midst of the
growing coarseness and frivolity of that century. At a
time when all the norms by which society checks the
individual were broken and no longer in force, the only
dignity possible was what one extracted from the depths
of one's own being. This necessarily implied a certain
exaggeration, even if only in defense against the orgiastic abandon of one's surroundings. Guizot, like Buster
Keaton, was the man who never laughs.[7] He never let
himself go. He was the outcome of several generations
of protestants of Nîmes, people who always watched
their step, never able to drift in their social environment,
never losing self-control. It had become an instinct with
them to interpret existence as resistance, digging one's
heels into the ground in order to stand against the cur-

---

[7] He tells Mme. de Gasparin with some satisfaction that the Pope, speaking to the French ambassador, had said in reference to him, Guizot: "He
is a great statesman. They say he never laughs." *Correspondance avec
Mme. de Gasparin*, p. 283.

rent. In a time like ours, all "currents" and abandon, it is good to put oneself in contact with men who refuse to be carried away. The Doctrinaires are an unusual case of intellectual responsibility, that is, of the quality most lacking to European intellectuals since 1750, and this lack is in turn one of the deepest causes of the disorder of the present.[8]

But I am not sure that my readers will be familiar with the achievement of the Doctrinaires, for scandalous as it may seem, there is not a single book that tries to give a precise idea of their thought,[9] nor, incredibly, even any fairly serious book on Guizot or Royer-Collard.[10] True, neither of them ever published a sonnet. But, after all, they thought, they thought deeply, originally, about the most serious problems of European public life and they built up the most admirable political theory of the entire century. It would be impossible to reconstruct the history of that century without an intimate knowledge of their attitude towards the major ques-

---

8 *Vide* the author's *Discourse on Intellectual Responsibility.*

9 The reader who looks for information on the subject will repeatedly come up against the evasive statement that the Doctrinaires had no identical theory, but differed among themselves. As if this were not what happened in any intellectual school and were not the most important difference between a group of men and a group of victrolas.

10 In the last few years M. Charles H. Pouthas has assumed the tiresome task of going through Guizot's archives and presenting a series of volumes, containing material without which it would be impossible to undertake the later work of reconstruction. On Royer-Collard there is not even this. One will find that eventually one has to fall back on Faguet's studies on the ideas of the two men. There is nothing better, and these studies, though extremely lively, are wholly inadequate.

tions of their time.[11] Their intellectual style is not only different in kind but seems another species, another essence than those that have triumphed in Europe both before and since. It is for this reason that in spite of their classic clarity they have not been understood, and yet it is quite possible that the future will belong to intellectual tendencies very similar to theirs. At least I can guarantee unexpected pleasures of the mind and an insight into social and political affairs wholly out of the ordinary to anyone who proposes to make a precise and systematic formulation of the ideas of the Doctrinaires. It was they who kept alive the best rationalist tradition, by which man dedicates himself to the search for absolutes, but unlike the lymphatic rationalism of the Encyclopedists and Revolutionaries—who find the absolute in abstractions at a dime the dozen—the Doctrinaires perceived the true absolute in history itself. History is the reality of man. He has no other. Through history he

11 For example, one cannot with a clear conscience—if by conscience we mean intellectual "conscience"—interpret the policy of resistance as pure and simple conservatism. It is entirely too obvious that Guizot, Royer-Collard, Broglie were not ordinary conservatives. The word "resistance"— which appearing in the above quotation from Ranke points to the influence of Guizot on that great historian—takes on a new meaning and suddenly, as it were, reveals its inmost being when we read in a speech by Royer-Collard: "Civil liberties are nothing but resistances." (*Vide* Barante: *La vie et les discours de Royer-Collard*, II, 130.) Here again we find European thinking at its best reducing statics to dynamics. The *state* of liberty results from a plurality of forces mutually resistant. But the speeches of Royer-Collard are so little read today that it will seem almost an impertinence to say that they are marvelous, that to read them is a pure intellectual delight, amusing, and even exhilarating, and that they represent the last example of the finest Cartesian style.

has made himself such as he is. To deny the past is foolish and illusory for the past is man's nature, of which
Boileau said that "if you drive it out, it will return at a
gallop." The past is not there, it has not taken the trouble
to pass, so that we may deny it but so that we may in-
tegrate it.[12] The Doctrinaires despised the "rights of
man" as metaphysical absolutes, abstractions and un-
realities, and considered man's real rights to be those
that are actually here, having appeared and consolidated
themselves, such as "liberties," lawfulness, magistracy,
"capacities." If they were alive today they would recognize the right of the strike (nonpolitical) and of collective bargaining. All this would seem obvious to an Eng-
lishman, but we of the continent, who perhaps since the
time of Alcuin have been about fifty years behind the
English, have not yet reached that stage.

The collectivists of today suffer from a similar igno-
rance of the old school of liberalism when they assume
offhand, as an indisputable fact, that it was individual-
istic. On all these subjects, as I have said, the ideas of
the time are hopelessly muddled. In recent years the
Russians have been in the habit of calling Russia "the
Collective." Would it not be interesting to find out what
ideas or images this word conjures up in the somewhat

12 *Vide* p. 221.

hazy brain of the Russian, who so often, like the Italian captain mentioned by Goethe, *"Bisogna aver una confusione nella testa"?* In view of all this I should like to ask the reader to consider, not in order to accept them but only to discuss them before passing judgment, the following theses:

1: Individualist liberalism is of the flora of the eighteenth century; it inspired, in part, the legislation of the French Revolution but it died with that event.

2: The characteristic creation of the nineteenth century was precisely collectivism. It was the first idea invented by that century, almost at birth, and it grew throughout its hundred years to the point of flooding the entire horizon.

3: This idea was of French origin, first appearing with the archreactionaries de Bonald and de Maistre. It was immediately accepted, in essence, by everyone but Benjamin Constant, a "hangover" from the preceding century. But it triumphed in Saint-Simon, Ballanche, Comte, and spread its seed to every corner of society.[13]

---

[13] The Germans claim to have discovered social reality as distinct from and "previous" to the individual, and consider the *Volksgeist* one of their most indigenous ideas. This is one of the cases that call particularly for the minute study of Franco-Germanic intellectual interchange between 1790 and 1830, to which I have referred in a previous footnote. The term *Volksgeist* reminds one of Voltaire's *esprit des nations*. The mainly French origin of collectivism is not an accident, having to do with the same causes that made France the cradle of sociology and of its rebirth around 1890 (Durkheim).

For example, a doctor in Lyons, M. Amard, will speak in 1821 of "collectivism" as opposed to "personalism." [14] As further evidence one may read the articles published in *L'Avenir* in 1830 and 1831 against individualism.

But there is something of even greater importance to be considered. When, proceeding through the century, we reach the great theorists of liberalism—John Stuart Mill and Spencer—we are surprised to find that their supposed defense of the individual is based not on the question of whether liberty is of profit or advantage to the individual, but, on the contrary, on whether it is of profit or advantage to society. The aggressive-looking title that Spencer chose for his book—*The Man versus the State*—has caused a good deal of willful misunderstanding among those who go no farther in a book than the title. Actually, as used in this title, the terms "man" and "state" mean simply two organs of the same subject —society—and the matter of discussion is whether certain social needs are best served by one organ or the other. That is all. Spencer's famous "individualism" is continually at odds with the collectivist atmosphere of his sociology. Fundamentally both he and John Stuart

---

[14] Vide *Doctrine de Saint-Simon* with introduction and notes by C. Bouglé and E. Halévy (p. 204, footnote). Written in 1829, this exposition of Saint-Simonism is one of the greatest works of the century. The accumulation of research in the notes by MM. Bouglé and Halévy makes it as well one of the most important contributions I know of to the understanding of the European mind between 1800 and 1830.

Mill treat the individual with the same socializing cruelty that termites display towards certain of their fellow beings, fattening them in order later to suck out their substance. For both, the collective was the real basis, the platform for the ingenuous dance of their ideas.

It should therefore be clear that my chivalric defense of the "old liberals" is entirely gratuitous and disinterested. For I am not one of the "old liberals." The discovery—an essential and glorious one—of the social or collective life was still too recent at that time. These men of the old school felt rather than understood the fact of collectivity, as distinct from individuals and not made up simply of their sum total, but they had no clear perception of its substance and attributes. Besides, it was then in the interest of the collectivity to concentrate on fattening the individual, and its features were therefore camouflaged by the social phenomena of the time. The hour of leveling, of spoils and redistribution in every sphere of life, had not yet sounded.

The "old liberals" therefore took no special precautions against collectivism, breathing it in with the very air around them. But when one has seen not only the good but also the terror and frightfulness of this social phenomenon, the plain fact of collectivity per se, one can only adhere to an entirely new kind of liberalism, less naïve, more skillful in its encounters, a liberalism that will soon be coming into its own and that even now can be distinguished on the horizon.

It would have been unnatural, nevertheless, for men so farsighted not to have glimpsed now and then the anguish that their time was holding in store for ours. General opinion to the contrary, predictions of the future have been normal enough in history.[15] In the work of Macaulay, Tocqueville, Comte we find our own time outlined in advance, and consider, for example, what John Stuart Mill was writing almost eighty years ago:

"Apart from the peculiar tenets of individual thinkers, there is also in the world at large an increasing inclination to stretch unduly the powers of society over the individual, both by the force of opinion and even by that of legislation; and as the tendency of all the changes taking place in the world is to strengthen society, and diminish the power of the individual, this encroachment is not one of the evils which tend spontaneously to disappear, but, on the contrary, to grow more and more formidable. The disposition of mankind, whether as rulers or as fellow citizens, to impose their own opinions and inclinations as a rule of conduct on others, is so energetically supported by some of the best and by some of the worst feelings incident to human nature, that it is hardly ever kept under restraint by anything but want of power; and as the power is not declining, but growing, unless a strong barrier of moral conviction can be raised against the mischief, we must expect, in the present circumstances of the world, to see it increase." (John Stuart Mill, *On Liberty*, London, 1913, p. 8.)

[15] An easy and useful job that someone ought to undertake would be to collect the predictions of the near future that have been made in every period of history. I have gathered enough to be amazed by the fact that there have always been a few men who were able to foresee the future.

But of greater interest to us in Mill is his anxiety over the pernicious kind of homogeneity that he saw growing throughout the West. It was this that moved him to seek refuge in a great thought expressed by Humboldt in his youth, that if mankind is to be enriched, to consolidate and perfect itself, there must exist a "variety of situations." [16] Within each nation and in the aggregate of nations there must be a diversity of circumstances, so that when one possibility fails others remain open. It is sheer madness to stake all Europe on one card, on a single type of man, on one identical "situation." Europe's secret talent up to the present day has been to avoid this, and it is the consciousness of this secret that has shaped the speech, sometimes stammering to be sure, of the perpetual liberalism of Europe. This consciousness includes a recognition of the plurality of Europe as a positive value in its own right, not evil but good. I have gone to some length to clarify this point so as to avoid any misunderstanding of the idea of a European supernation set forth in this book.

The course on which we are now embarked, with its progressive lessening of the "variety of situations," leads us directly back to the Lower Empire, also a period of masses and of frightful homogeneity. As early as in the time of the Antonines there had become apparent a

[16] *Gesammelte Schriften,* vol. 1, p. 106.

strange phenomenon that has been less stressed and analyzed than it deserves: men had become stupid. The process had its roots farther back. The Stoic Posidonius, Cicero's teacher, is supposed with some reason to have been the last of the ancients capable of facing facts with an open and active mind, willing to submit them to investigation. After him heads fell into disuse, and except among the Alexandrians they did nothing but repeat, stereotype.

But this form of life that spread throughout the Empire, both homogeneous and stupid—and one by virtue of the other—has left its most terrible symptom and record where one would least expect it and where, as far as I know, no one has looked for it: in the language. Language, which fails us in our common needs of expression, reveals and even trumpets forth against our will the inmost condition of the society by which it is spoken. The language in use among the non-Hellenized part of the Roman people was the so-called "vulgar Latin," matrix of our Romance languages. We know little of this vulgar Latin and our idea of it comes largely from reconstruction, but we know enough, and more than enough, to be appalled by two of its characteristics. One is its incredible simplicity of grammar in comparison with classical Latin. The exquisite Indo-European complexity that had been preserved in the language of the upper classes was replaced by plebeian speech, of easy structure but at the same time, and for that very reason, ponderously mechanical, uncouth: a stammering, periphrastic speech, struggling and round-about like that of a child. It is a puerile language that allows for neither the fine edge of reason nor the shimmer of lyricism, a sad and groping language, soulless, without warmth or light. The words resemble old copper coins, filthy and chipped, as if weary of rolling through all the hovels of the Mediterranean. What lives emptied of themselves, desolate, condemned to an eternal day-to-day, one glimpses behind this dry linguistic apparatus!

The other terrifying characteristic of vulgar Latin is precisely its homogeneity. Linguists, who next to aviators are perhaps the least fainthearted of men, seem unperturbed by the fact that the same language should have been spoken in countries as unlike as Carthage and Gaul, Tingis and Dalmatia, Hispania and Rumania. But I who am somewhat timid, and tremble to see weeds troubled by the wind, cannot help shuddering before this fact. It seems to me simply atrocious. To be sure, I try to picture the "inside" of what seems, viewed from without, plain homogeneity; I try to discover the living reality of which this fact is the immobile stamp. Obviously there were variations: Africanisms, Hispanicisms, Gallicisms, but this is only another way of saying that the trunk of the language was common and identical, in spite of the distances, the rarity of interchange, the difficulty of communication, and the absence of any literature that would have tended to fix its forms. And how could these various people have become equivalent, the Celt and the Belgian, the inhabitant of Hippo and that of Lutetia, the Mauretanian and the Dacian, if not by virtue of a general flattening that had reduced existence to its common denominator and nullified their lives? Vulgar Latin lies like a ghastly petrification in our archives, testifying that history once struggled for its life beneath the homogeneous empire of vulgarity, because of the disappearance of a fruitful "variety of situations."

IV

Neither this essay nor I are engaged in politics. The matter under discussion here is previous to politics and springs from its subsoil. My work is the obscure, subterranean task of a miner. The job of the so-called intellectual is in a certain sense opposed to that of the politician, the former aiming, often in vain, to clarify things a little whereas the politician usually adds to the confusion. Aligning oneself with the left, as with the right, is only one of the numberless ways open to man of being an imbecile: both are forms of moral hemiplegia. Furthermore, the persistence of these terms helps not a little to falsify the already false "reality" of the present, for the circle of political experiences to which they correspond is closed, as witnessed by the fact that today we are offered a prospect of tyranny from the left while the right promises revolution.

There is no question but that one must deal with the problems of the time. It is what I have been doing all my life; I have always, so to speak, been in the breach. But *they* are now saying—it is a "current"—that everyone, even at the cost of mental clarity, should be involved in politics *sensu stricto*. It is said, of course, by those who have nothing else to do, and they even go so far as to corroborate it by quoting Pascal's imperative of stupidity; but I have long since learned, as a measure of elementary hygiene, to be on guard when anyone quotes Pascal.

Total politicalism, the absorption of everything and of the entire man by politics, is one and the same phenomenon as the revolt of the masses. The mass in revolt has lost all capacity for knowledge or devotion. It can contain nothing but politics, a raving, frenetic, exorbitant politics that claims to replace all knowledge, religion, wisdom—everything, in short, really qualified to occupy the center of the human mind. Politics drains men of solitude and intimacy, and preaching total politicalism is therefore one of the techniques of socialization.

When someone asks us where we stand politically, or

anticipating, with the usual impertinence of the time, ascribes us to one party or another, instead of answering we should cross-examine the inquirer: what does he think of man and nature and history? what is his understanding of society, the individual, collectivity, the state, custom, law? Politics hurries to put out the light so that all these cats will be gray. These are the subjects with which European thought must cope. It is there for that purpose, not to play the peacock at academic meetings. It must cast new light on them and soon; or at least it must, as Dante said, find the path before it is too late:

> . . . studiate il passo
> Mentre que l'Occidente non s'annera.
> (*Purg.* XXVII, 62–63.)

It is from this alone that one might hope, with some slight chance of success, for a solution to the tremendous problem posed by the masses of the present time.

I have tried to give a first approximation to it in my earlier book, *The Revolt of the Masses.* In order to deal with the problem more seriously and profoundly one has no alternative but to put on a diving suit and descend to the farthest depth of man. It is a task to be undertaken earnestly and without pretensions, and it is what I have attempted in a book to be published soon under the title *Man and People.*

It is when one has really understood the make-up of this

human type dominant today, and that I have called the mass-man, that the more fruitful and dramatic questions arise: can this type of man be reformed? I mean the serious faults that he harbors, so serious that if they are not plucked out they must cause the annihilation of the West —can these be corrected? For as the reader will see, we are dealing with a man hermetically sealed, not open to any higher appeal.

The other decisive question, on which in my opinion all possibility of health depends, is this: can the masses, even if they want to, be awakened to the personal life? This formidable subject is still too untouched to be developed here; the terms in which it must be posed hardly exist as yet in the public consciousness. Nor has there been any approach to a study of the distinct margin of individuality that each period bequeaths to human existence, a study that would be of vital importance. For it is pure mental inertia to assume according to the theory of "progressism"—and its advocate, Herbert Spencer, who was a good engineer but no historian—that the frame allowed to man for the functioning of his personality grows with the progress of history. No: history is full of recoils in this sphere, and it may well be that the structure of modern life is a supreme impediment to man's living as an individual.

When I consider the great cities with their immense

agglomerations of human beings coming and going in the streets, gathering for celebrations or political demonstrations, there is one thought that takes hold of me almost to the point of obsession: how would a man of twenty today go about planning a life that would have a form peculiar to himself and that would therefore have to be realized by his own efforts and his own independent initiative? As he tries to unfold this picture in his mind, will he not become aware that if not impossible it is at least highly improbable, because there is no room for him to move according to the dictates of his own will? He will soon notice that his plan bumps against that of his neighbor, that his neighbor's life is pressing against his. With the ease of adaptation proper to his age, he will be driven by discouragement to give up not only all action but any personal desires as well, and will look for the opposite solution: he will imagine a standard life, made up of *desiderata* common to all, and he will realize that the only way of achieving it is to ask for it or demand it collectively with others. Hence mass action.

It is horrible, but I think I have not exaggerated the situation in which almost all Europeans are beginning to find themselves. Imagine a cell so overcrowded with prisoners that no one can move an arm or leg without jostling the bodies of the others. In such a situation movements have to be carried out in common and even the respiratory muscles must work to an ordered rhythm. This is what Europe would be turned into, an anthill. But not even this cruel picture is a solution. The human anthill is impossible because it is through what is known as individualism that the world, and every man in the world, have been enriched, and it is this enrichment that has so fabulously multiplied the human plant. Were the remains of this "individualism" to vanish, the gigantic famine of the Lower Empire would reappear in Europe and the anthill would succumb as at the breath of an angry and vengeful god. There would be left far less men, but men who would be a little more worthy of the name.

Before the fierce pathos of this question, which is already in sight whether we will or no, the theme of "social justice," for all its respectability, pales and shrinks until it resembles the false, rhetorical sigh of romanticism. But the question also brings into orientation ways of achieving whatever is possible and just in this "social justice," ways that seem not to pass through a wretched socialization but to lead directly to a generous "solidarism." The word is weak because it has not yet been filled out with a strong system of social and historical ideas and so smells only of vague philanthropies.

The first condition for improving the present situation, and the only thing that will enable us to attack the evil at the deep levels from which it springs, is an awareness of its enormous difficulty. We must realize that it is very hard to save a civilization when its hour has come to fall beneath the power of demagogues. For the demagogue has been the great strangler of civilization. Both Greek and Roman civilizations fell at the hands of this loathsome creature who brought from Macaulay the remark that "in every century the vilest examples of human nature have been among demagogues." [17] But a man is not a demagogue simply because he stands up and shouts at the crowd. There are times when this can be a hallowed office. The real demagogy of the demagogue is in his mind and is rooted in his irresponsibility towards the ideas that he handles—ideas not of his own creation, but which he has only taken over from their true creators. Demagogy is a form of intellectual degeneration, which as a sweeping phenomenon of European history first appeared in France around 1750.[18] Why then? Why in France? This is one of the vital points in the destiny of the West and especially in that of France.

The fact is that from then on it was the general belief in France—and this belief spread through almost the entire continent—that the only method of solving great human problems was the method of revolution, meaning by

[17] *History of England from the Accession of James II.* New York: Harper & Brothers, 1856, vol. I, p. 547.
[18] I have ventured a few remarks on this subject in my "Discourse on Intellectual Responsibility."

this what Leibnitz called "general revolution," [19] the will to change everything at a single blow and in all spheres of life.[20] It is thanks to this that that marvel, France, has arrived in such a bad state at the difficult conjuncture of the present. For that country has, or thinks that it has, a revolutionary tradition, and if it is bad enough to be revolutionary, how much worse is it to be so, paradoxically, by tradition! It is true that France has had one Great Revolution and several that were grim or ridiculous, but if we stick to the bare truth of the records we see that the main result of those revolutions was that for a century—with the exception of a few days or weeks—the political forms of France, more than those of any other country, were to a greater or less extent authoritarian and counterrevolutionary. It is particularly clear that the great moral bog of French history, the twenty years of the Second Empire, was above all due to the buffooneries of the revolutionists of 1848,[21] many of whom were ad-

[19] "*Je trouve même que des opinions approchantes s'insinuant peu à peu dans l'esprit des hommes du grand monde, que règlent les autres et dont dépendent les affaires, et, se glissant dans les livres à la mode, disposent toutes choses à la révolution générale dont l'Europe est menacée.*" (*Nouveaux essais sur l'entendement humain*, livre IV, ch. 16.) This shows two things: (1) that at the time when Leibnitz wrote this, around 1700, someone was able to foresee what actually happened a century later; (2) that the evils from which Europe is now suffering have more profound origins, chronologically and vitally, than is commonly supposed.

[20] "*. . . notre siècle qui se croit destiné à changer les lois en tout genre . . .*" D'Alembert. "*Discours préliminaire à l'Encyclopédie,*" *Œuvres*, 1821, vol. 1, p. 56.

[21] "*Cette honnête, irréprochable, mais imprévoyante et superficielle révolution de 1848 eut pour conséquence, au bout de moins d'un an, de donner le pouvoir a l'élément le plus pesant, le moins clairvoyant, le plus ob-*

mitted by Raspail himself to have been his former clients.

In revolutions the abstract tries to rebel against the concrete; failure is therefore of the very substance of revolutions. Human affairs, unlike problems of astronomy or chemistry, are not abstract. They are historical and therefore in the highest degree concrete. The only method of thinking about them with some chance of hitting the mark is "historic reason." Looking back over the political life of France in the last hundred and fifty years one is struck by the fact that her geometricians, physicists, doctors have almost always been wrong in their political judgments, whereas the historians have seldom missed. But physico-mathematical rationalism has been too glorified in France not to have tyrannized public opinion. Witness Malebranche's breaking with a friend on whose table he found a volume of Thucydides.[22]

In my exile in France, wandering alone through the streets of Paris, I came to realize that I really know no one in that great city but the statues. Among these at least I found old friends who had stimulated or had been the lasting masters of my inner life, and having no one

stinément conservateur de notre pays." Renan, *Questions Contemporaines,* Renan, who had been young in 1848 and had sympathized with that movement, felt obliged in his mature years to make certain reservations in its favor, assuming that it had been "honorable and irreproachable."

[22] *Vide* R. Carré, *La philosophie de Fontenelle,* p. 143.

else to talk to it was with them that I discussed the great
problems of mankind. Perhaps some day I will publish
these "Conversations with Statues" that so sweetened a
painful and sterile stage of my life. In one I reasoned
with the Marquis de Condorcet, on the Quai Conti, on
the dangerous concept of progress. With the little bust of
Comte, in his apartment in the Rue Monsieur le Prince,
I spoke of "spiritual power," wielded so inadequately
by literary mandarins and by a university out of joint
with the real life of nations. I also had the honor of carrying a message from this bust to the large one in the
Place de la Sorbonne, the bust of the false Comte, the
official one, the Comte de Littré. But of course my greatest interest was in listening once again to the man to
whom Europe owes the most, our great master Descartes.

The cards of my life have so fallen that quite by
chance I am writing these lines in Holland, within sight
of the place that in 1642 was the home of the new dis-
coverer of "reason." This place, called Endegeest, whose
trees shade my window, is now an insane asylum. Twice
a day I see the idiots and the demented pass menacingly
near, refreshing their worn-out humanity for a little
while in the open air.

Our three centuries of experience with "rationalism"
force us to take new stock of the glory and limitations of
that prodigious Cartesian "reason." It is a system of

thought purely mathematical, physical, biological. Its extraordinary triumphs over nature, beyond anything that had been dreamed, only underline further its failure in the realm of strictly human affairs and demand that it be integrated in the more deep-rooted system of "historic reason." [23]

The latter shows us the futility of all general revolution, of all attempts—such as that of the Confusionists of '89—to bring about a sudden change of society and begin history anew. It opposes to the method of revolution the only method worthy of the long experience that lies behind the European of today. Revolutions, so incontinent in their hypocritically generous haste to proclaim the rights of man, have always violated, trampled on, and broken man's most fundamental right, so fundamental that it may stand as the definition of his being: the right to continuity. The only radical difference between human history and "natural history" is that the former can never begin again. Koehler and others have shown that the chimpanzee and the orangutan are distinguished from man not by what is known strictly speaking as intelligence, but because they have far less memory. Every morning the poor beasts have to face almost total oblivion of what they lived through the day before, and their intellect has to work with a minimum fund of experience.

[23] *Vide* "History as a System."

Similarly, the tiger of today is identical with that of six thousand years ago, each one having to begin his life as a tiger from the beginning as if none had ever existed before him. But man, thanks to his power of memory, accumulates his past; he possesses it and can make use of it. Man is never the first man but begins his life on a certain level of accumulated past. That is his single treasure, his mark and privilege. And the important part of this treasure is not what seems to us correct and worth preserving, but the memory of mistakes, allowing us not to repeat the same ones forever. Man's real treasure is the treasure of his mistakes, piled up stone by stone through thousands of years. It is because of this that Nietzsche defined man as the being "with the longest memory." Breaking the continuity with the past, wanting to begin again, is a lowering of man and a plagiarism of the orangutan. It was a Frenchman, Dupont-White, who around 1860 had the courage to exclaim: "Continuity is one of the rights of man; it is a homage of everything that distinguishes him from the beast." [24]

When at the coronation of King George VI the English people gave unusual solemnity to the rite of coronation, they affirmed, in face of the turmoil on the continent, the permanent standards that govern their life. As always,

[24] In his Preface to the translation of *Liberty* by John Stuart Mill, p. 44.

they have given us a lesson. For the history of Europe
presents the picture of a bustling throng of peoples, full
of genius but without serenity, never mature, always adolescent, with behind them, in the background, England—
the nurse of Europe. It is said that for a long time the
British monarchy has been a merely symbolic institution.
This is quite true, but the phrase leaves its finest aspect
out of account. Actually the monarchy fulfills no material, tangible function in the British Empire; it is not its
role to govern, nor to administer justice, nor to command the army; but this does not make it an empty and
useless institution. The British monarchy fulfills a highly
determined and effective function: that of symbolizing.

England is the country that has always reached the
future first, leading the others in almost every sphere of
life. We might omit the "almost." And now this same
people, not without a little of the pure impertinence of
the dandy, forces us to witness an age-old ceremonial
and to see in action—for they have never ceased to be
actual—the oldest and most magical tools in its history,
the crown and scepter, which with us rule nothing but
the luck in a pack of cards. With such gestures the English persist in proving to us that their past, precisely because it is past, because they themselves experienced it,
still exists for them. From a future which we have not

yet reached they show us a past in full force.[25] They circulate through their whole history, they are the true masters, the actual possessors of their centuries. And this is what it means to be a people of men: to be able to continue one's yesterday today without thereby ceasing to live for tomorrow; to live in the real present, since the present is only the presence of past and future, the place where the past and the future actually exist.

Through the symbolic rites of coronation England has once more opposed to the revolutionary method the method of continuity, the only one that can avoid, in the course of human affairs, that pathological element that makes history a notorious, constant struggle between paralytics and epileptics.

[25] This is not simply a figure of speech but literally true, since it applies where the words "in force" have the most immediate meaning, that is, in law. In England there is "no barrier between the past and the present. Practical law can be traced back through history with no discontinuity to times immemorial. Juridically speaking, there is no such thing as 'ancient English law.' In England, therefore, all law is modern, no matter what its age." Lévy-Ullmann, *Le Système Juridique de l'Angleterre*, vol. 1, pp. 38–39.

3

Man the Technician

A SUBJECT to be ardently discussed in the coming years is that of the advantages, the threat, and the limitation of technology. I have always considered it the task of the writer to foresee in leisurely anticipation the problems which will be confronting his readers in days to come, and to provide them in time, i. e., before the discussion opens, with clear ideas about the question, so as to enable them to enter the fray with the serene mind of people who, in principle, see the solution. *"On ne doit écrire que pour faire connaître la vérité,"* said Malebranche, turning his back on literature of fiction. Consciously or not, Western man years ago gave up expecting anything of such writings; he thirsts and hungers for clear and distinct ideas about those things that really matter.

Here, then, we are embarked on the altogether unliterary undertaking of finding an answer to the question: what is technology? The first attack on our problem will still be awkward and at long range.

When winter comes man is cold, and this "being cold" contains two disparate ingredients. One is the fact that he encounters around him the reality called cold, the other that this reality is offensive to him, that it impresses him as negative. What does this negative mean? It is clear. Let us take the extreme case. The cold is such that man feels he is dying, that is, he feels that it is killing him. But man does not want to die; normally he clings to survival. We are so wont to find in ourselves and our fellow men this desire to persist, to affirm ourselves in the face of all negative circumstances, that it costs us a certain effort to realize that there is something strange about it. To ask why a man would rather live than die seems absurd and naïve. Yet it is one of the most justified and sensible questions we can ask. It is customary to answer it by talking of the instinct of self-preservation. Now in the first place, the concept of instinct is in itself highly obscure and not at all illuminating; and secondly, even if it were clear it is well known that in man the instincts are as good as eliminated. Man does not live by his instincts, but governs himself by means of other faculties, such as will and thought, which control his instincts. Proof of this is given by the resolve of those people who prefer death to life and, for whatever reason, suppress in themselves the presumed instinct of self-preservation.

The explanation through instinct fails. With or without it, the fact remains that man persists in living because he wants to and that for this reason he feels the necessity of avoiding the cold and procuring warmth for himself. The lightning of an autumnal thunderstorm may set the woods on fire, whereupon man will draw near to warm himself at the beneficent glow chance has given him. Thus he meets his necessity by simply availing himself of a fire he has come upon. (I make due apology for uttering so trite a remark; unfortunately, I see no way of being spared, at the outset, this humiliation; but to be caught at platitudes one does not even understand would be the last straw, and not uncommon either.) So that the act of warming himself now is reduced to the performance of an activity with which man finds himself endowed by nature, viz., the capacity of walking and thus approaching the source of heat. In other cases warmth may be supplied not by a fire, but by a cave in a near-by mountain.

Another necessity of man is to feed himself, and this he does by eating fruits gathered from trees and shrubs or edible roots or such animals as fall into his hands. Another necessity is to drink. And so forth.

The satisfaction of these needs imposes a new need: to move about in space, to walk; that is, to reduce distances. And since it may be necessary to do this as fast as possible, man has to reduce time, to gain time. When attacked by an enemy—a wild beast or another man— he must flee, i. e., cover much ground in the shortest time possible. Proceeding in this way we should, with a little patience, arrive at a definition of the system of necessities under which man finds himself, much in the same way as he finds himself equipped with a certain stock of activities —walking, eating, warming himself—which meet these necessities.

Obvious though all this sounds—I repeat, it makes me blush to propound it—we must dwell upon the meaning the term "necessity" has here. What does it mean that, to be warm, to be fed, to walk, are necessities of man? Undoubtedly this: that they are necessary natural conditions of life. Man is aware of their material or objective "necessariness" and therefore feels them subjectively as necessities. But, be it noted, their necessariness is purely conditional. The stone suspended in the air falls necessarily, with a categorical and unconditional necessity. But man may decide against meeting his need—of food, for instance, as Mahatma Gandhi does from time to time. Feeding, we observe, is not necessary in itself; it is necessary "for" living. It has the same degree of necessity as has living "if" there is to be living. Hence, living is the original necessity of which all others are mere consequences. Now, as I said above, man lives because he wants to. The necessity of living is not imposed on him by force as the incapability of destroying itself is imposed on matter. Life—necessity of necessities—is necessary only in a subjective sense: simply because of man's peremptory resolve to live. Its necessity arises from an act of the will—an act into the meaning and origin of which we shall look no further, taking it as a crude fact to start from. For whatever reasons, man happens to have a keen desire to go on living, to "be in the world," although he is the sole known being endowed with the faculty—such a strange, paradoxical, frightening faculty from the ontological or metaphysical point of view—of annihilating himself and voluntarily renouncing his existence in the world.

So ardent is this desire that, when he is unable to satisfy his vital necessities because nature does not grant him the indispensable means, man will not resign himself. If, for lack of fire or a cave, he is unable to perform the act of warming himself, or for lack of fruits, roots, animals he is unable to eat, man mobilizes a second line of activities. He lights a fire, he builds a house, he tills and hunts. These necessities, it is true, and the activities that satisfy them directly—by using means which if they are there at all are there already—are common to both men and animals. The one thing we cannot be sure of is whether the animal has the same desire to live as man. This much, however, is certain: the animal, when it cannot satisfy its vital needs —when there is neither fire nor a cave, for example— does nothing about it and lets itself die. Man, on the contrary, comes forward with a new type of activity; he produces what he does not find in nature, whether because it does not exist at all or because it is not to hand when he needs it. Thus he lights a fire, he makes a cave, that is, a house, if these are not available in his setting; he rides a horse or builds an automobile to gain time and space. Be it well noted: making a fire is an act very different from keeping warm; tilling is not feeding; constructing an automobile is not walking. Now it becomes clear why I had to insist on the hackneyed definition of keeping warm, feeding, moving about in space.

Kindling a fire, plowing, manufacturing an automobile are not activities with which we satisfy our necessities; on the contrary, their immediate effect is a suspension of the primary set of actions with which we meet needs directly. The ultimate aim of the secondary set of actions is the same as that of the original set; but—and this is the crucial point—it presupposes a capacity which man has, but which is lacking in animals. This capacity is not so much intelligence—about this point we shall say a word later; it is the possibility of disengaging oneself temporarily from the vital urgencies and remaining free for activities which in themselves are not satisfaction of needs. The animal is always and inextricably bound up with the former. Its existence is nothing but the whole collection of its elemental, i. e., organic or biological, necessities and the actions which meet them. This is life in the organic or biological sense of the word.

But can we really speak of necessities when referring to a being like this? When we used the concept of necessity with reference to man we understood by it the conditions he finds imposed upon himself "for" living. Hence, they are not his life; or to put it the other way round, his life does not coincide, at least not wholly, with the system of his organic necessities. If it did, he would not feel eating, drinking, keeping warm, etc., as necessities, as inexorable impositions laid upon his authentic being from without, which this being must needs reckon with but which do not constitute his true life. In this subjective sense an animal has no necessities. It may be hungry; but feeling hungry and looking for food cannot appear to it as a necessity imposed upon its authentic being, because there is nothing else for it to do. Man, on the other hand, if he succeeded in being without necessities and consequently without concern about satisfying them, would have enough left to do, a wide scope for living, in fact just those occupations and that kind of life which he regards as most human.

This, unexpectedly, reveals to us the strange constitution of man. While all other beings coincide with their objective conditions—with their nature or circumstance —man alone is different from, and alien to, his circumstance. Yet if he wants to exist in it, there is no way but to accept the conditions it imposes. Because man is not identical with his circumstance, but only embedded in it, he is able to rid himself of it in certain moments and retire into his inner self. In these intervals of extra- and supernatural existence, in which he withdraws from attending to his natural needs, he invents and carries out the second set of actions. He lights a fire, he builds a house, he cultivates the field, he designs an automobile.

All these actions have one trait in common. They presuppose and include the invention of a procedure which guarantees, within certain limits, that we can obtain at our pleasure and convenience the things we need but do not find in nature. Thereafter it no longer matters whether or not there is fire here and now; we make it, that is to say, we perform a certain set of actions that we invent once and for all. They frequently consist in manufacturing an object which, by simply operating, procures what we need; we call it the tool or implement.

From which follows that these actions modify and reform nature, creating in it objects which had not existed before, either not at all or not where and when they were needed. Here, then, we have at last the so-called technical acts which are exclusively human. In their entirety these acts constitute technology, which may now be defined as the improvement brought about on nature by man for the satisfaction of his necessities. The necessities, we saw, are imposed on man by nature; man answers by imposing changes on nature. Thus technology is man's reaction upon nature or circumstance. It leads to the construction of a new nature, a supernature interposed between man and original nature. Be it noted therefore: technology is not man's effort to satisfy his natural necessities. This definition would be equivocal, since it would hold likewise for the biological complex of animal actions. Technology is a reform of nature, of that nature which makes us needy and necessitous, a reform in the sense of abolishing necessities as such by guaranteeing their satisfaction under all circumstances. If nature automatically lit a fire for us as soon as we were cold, we should be unaware of the necessity of keeping warm, as we normally are unaware of the necessity of breathing and simply breathe without any problem. In fact, this is what technology does for us. It immediately meets the sensation of cold with heat and thereby rids it of its grim, dismal, negative character.

This, then, is the first clumsy approximation to an

answer for the question: what is technology? From now on things will be more intricate and, accordingly, more amusing.

II BEING AND WELL-BEING——THE "NECESSITY" OF DRUNKENNESS——THE SUPERFLUOUS IS THE NECESSARY——RELATIVITY OF TECHNOLOGY

Technology, in contrast to the adaptation of the individual to the medium, is the adaptation of the medium to the individual. This alone should be enough for us to surmise that we might be dealing here with a movement contrary to all biological movements.

To react upon his environment, not to resign himself to the world as it is——that is the token of man. Even when studying him from the zoological point of view we feel assured of his presence as soon as we find nature altered, e. g., when we come upon stones hewn to the shape of implements. Man without technology——that is, without reaction upon his medium——is not man.

Up to this point, we have been regarding technology as a reaction to organic and biological necessities. We insisted on a precise definition of the term "necessity." Feeding, we said, is a necessity, because it is an indispensable condition of living and man apparently has a keen desire to live. To live, to "be in the world," we recognized as the necessity of necessities.

But technology is not restricted to the satisfaction of necessities. As old as the invention of tools and procedures for keeping warm, feeding, etc., are many others serving to procure obviously unnecessary objects and situations. As old and as widespread as the act of lighting a fire, for instance, is that of getting drunk. I mean to say the use of substances and procedures which produce a psychophysical state of delightful exaltation or delightful stupor. The drug is as early an invention as any. So much so, in fact, that it is even open to discussion whether fire was invented primarily for the purpose of avoiding the cold—an organic necessity and a *sine qua non* of life —or of getting drunk. We know of primitive tribes who light a fire in a cave which makes them sweat so profusely that, from the combined smoke and excessive heat, they fall into a swoon akin to drunkenness. These are the so-called sweathouses.

There are endless ways of producing delightful visions or conveying intense bodily pleasures. Notable among the latter is the kat of Yemen and Ethiopia, a substance which affects the prostate and thereby makes walking increasingly gratifying the longer it is done. Among ecstasy-producing drugs we have belladonna, Jimson weed, the Peruvian coca, etc.

Let us mention in this context that ethnologists disagree as to whether the most archaic form of the bow is that of an instrument for war and the hunt or that of a musical instrument. We need not now decide this question. What interests us is the fact that the musical bow, whether it be the original bow or not, appears among the most primitive instruments.

These facts reveal that primitive man feels pleasurable states of mind to be as necessary as the satisfaction of his minimum needs. Thus it seems that, from the very beginning, the concept of "human necessity" comprises indiscriminately what is objectively necessary and what is objectively superfluous. Were we to decide which of our needs are strictly necessary and which we can go without, we should be in a pretty quandary. It would soon become patent that man has an incredibly elastic attitude towards those necessities which, *a priori*, would seem the most elemental and indispensable, such as food, heat, etc. Not only upon compulsion, but even from sheer zest, he reduces his food to a minimum and trains himself to stand amazingly low temperatures; whereas certain superfluous things he will give up very reluctantly or not at all, in extreme cases preferring to die rather than renounce them.

Whence we draw the conclusion that man's desire to live, to be in the world, is inseparable from his desire to live well. Nay more, he conceives of life not as simply being, but as well-being; and he regards the objective conditions of being as necessary only because being is the necessary condition of well-being. A man who is absolutely convinced that he cannot obtain, even approximately, what he calls well-being, and will have to put up with bare being, commits suicide. Not being, but well-being, is the fundamental necessity of man, the necessity of necessities.

Herewith we arrive at a concept of "human necessity" thoroughly different from that of our first definition and different also from that which, thanks to insufficient analysis and careless thinking, tends to be generally accepted. Such books on technology as I have read—all of them falling short of their great subject—are unaware that the concept of "human necessity" is fundamental for the understanding of technology. They all, as was to be expected, make use of this concept; but since they do not recognize that the whole problem hinges upon it, they take it as they find it in circulation in everyday thinking.

Let us, before proceeding, state briefly what we have found. Food, heat, etc., we have said, are human necessities because they are objective conditions of life understood as mere existence in the world; they are necessary according as man thinks it necessary to live. And man, we observe, clings to life. Now we recognize that this statement was equivocal. Man has no desire to "be in the world"; he wants to live well. Man is the animal that considers necessary only the objectively superfluous.

And to know this is essential for our comprehension of technology. Technology is the production of super-fluities—today as in the paleolithic age. That is why animals are atechnical; they are content with the simple act of living and with what is objectively required for it. From the point of view of bare living the animal is perfect and needs no technology. Man, technology, well-being are, in the last instance, synonymous. Only when we conceive of them as such are we able to grasp the meaning of technology as an absolute fact in the universe. If technology served but to take care more comfortably of the necessities of animal life, there would be a strange case of duplication. Two sets of acts—the instinctive acts of animals and the technical acts of man—would, despite their dissimilarity, serve the same purpose of sustaining organic life in the world. For, there is no getting around it, the animal fares perfectly well with its system which is by no means basically defective, neither more nor less defective, as a matter of fact, than that of man.

Everything becomes clear, however, when we realize that there are two purposes. One to sustain organic life, mere being in nature, by adapting the individual to the medium; the other to promote good life, well-being, by adapting the medium to the will of the individual.

Since human necessities are necessary only in connection with well-being, we cannot find out what they are unless we find out what man understands by well-being. And that complicates things immeasurably. For how shall we ever know all that man has understood, understands, and will understand by well-being, the necessity of necessities, the "one thing needful" of which Jesus spoke to Martha—Mary's being the true technology in his judgment.

Take Pompey, to whom what really mattered was not living but sailing the seven seas, once more flying the flag of the seafaring people of Miletus, the country of the *aei-nautei* (the eternal mariners) to whom Thales belonged and who had been the creators of a new bold commerce, a new bold policy, a new bold knowledge, Occidental science. Or take, on the one hand, the fakir, the ascetic, and, on the other, the sensualist, the pleasure lover! Whereas life in the biological sense is a fixed entity defined for each species once and for all, life in the human sense of good life is always mobile and infinitely variable. And with it, because they are a function of it, vary human necessities; and since technology is a system of actions called forth and directed by these necessities, it likewise is of Protean nature and ever changing.

It would be vain to attempt to study technology as though it were an independent entity; it is not directed by a single purpose known to us beforehand. The idea of progress, pernicious in all fields when applied without caution, has been disastrous here also. It assumes that man's vital desires are always the same and that the only thing that varies in the course of time is the progressive advance towards their fulfillment. But this is as wrong as wrong can be. The idea of human life, the profile of well-being, has changed countless times and sometimes so radically that definite technical advances were abandoned and their traces lost. In other cases, and they are almost the most frequent in history, invention and inventor were persecuted as immoral. The fact that we ourselves are urged on by an irresistible hunger for inventions does not justify the inference that it has always been thus. On the contrary, more often than not man has had a mysterious horror of discoveries, as though he felt lurking under their apparent beneficence the threat of a terrible danger. And we, amid all our enthusiasm for technical inventions, are we not beginning to experience something similar? It would be enormously and thrillingly instructive if somebody were to write a history of those technical achievements which, after having been attained and regarded as indelible acquisitions—*ktesis eis aei*—fell into oblivion and were completely lost.

III THE EFFORT TO SAVE EFFORT IS AN EFFORT
—THE PROBLEM OF SAVED EFFORT
—LIFE AS INVENTION

My book *The Revolt of the Masses* was written under the haunting impression—in 1928, be it noted, at the climax of prosperity—that this magnificent and miraculous technology of ours was endangered and might crumble between our fingers and vanish faster than anybody imagined. Today I am more than ever frightened. I wish it would dawn upon engineers that, in order to be an engineer, it is not enough to be an engineer. While they are minding their own business history may be pulling away the ground from under their feet.

Alertness is what we require. We are not allowed to confine ourselves within our own professions, but must live in full view of the entire scene of life, which is always total. The supreme art of living is a consummation gained by no single calling and no single science; it is the yield of all occupations and all sciences, and many things besides. It is an all-heeding circumspection. Human life and everything in it is a constant and absolute risk. The deadly blow may come from where it was least to be expected. A whole culture may run dry through an imperceptible leak. Even if the engineer puts aside forebodings, which after all are mere possibilities, what was his situation yesterday and what can he expect of tomorrow? This much is clear: the social, economic, and political conditions under which he works are changing rapidly.

Therefore we had better give up regarding technology as the one positive thing, the only immutable reality in the hands of man. Supposing the kind of well-being we seek today changed its character perceptibly, supposing the idea of life, which is the inspiring and directing force of all our actions, underwent some sort of mutation, would not our present technology be thrown out of gear and have to take new bearings according to our new desires?

People believe modern technology more firmly established in history than all previous technologies because of its scientific foundation. But this alleged security is illusory and the unquestionable superiority of modern technology as technology even implies an element of weakness. Since it is based on the exactness of science, it is dependent on more presuppositions and conditions and is, consequently, less spontaneous and self-reliant than earlier technologies.

Indeed, it is just this feeling of security which is endangering Western civilization. The belief in progress, the conviction that on this level of history a major setback can no longer happen and the world will mechanically go the full length of prosperity, has loosened the rivets of human caution and flung open the gates for a new invasion of barbarism.

For an example of the instability and diversity of technology consider that, at the time of Plato, Chinese technology was in many respects considerably superior to that of the Greeks; or that certain works of Egyptian engineers surpass even the miracles wrought by Western civilization—the lake of Moeris, for instance, which is mentioned by Herodotus and the ruins of which, after it had been believed a fable, were recently discovered. Owing to this gigantic power plant certain regions of the Nile valley, which today are desert, were once most fertile country.

It may be true that all technologies have in common a certain body of technical discoveries which has accumulated in spite of considerable losses and reverses. In this case it may be justified to speak of an absolute progress of technology; still, there always remains the danger lest the concept of absolute progress be defined from the standpoint of the person speaking. And this standpoint is, at best, not absolute. While the definer maintains it with blind faith, mankind may be preparing to abandon it.

We shall have a few more words to say about the different types of technology, their vicissitudes, their advantages, and their limitation. For the moment, we must not lose sight of the general idea of technology, for it encloses the most fascinating secrets.

Technical acts are not those through which we strive directly to satisfy our necessities, whether elemental or frankly superfluous, but those in which we first invent and then carry out a plan of action which permits us to achieve such satisfaction through the least effort possible and to secure completely new possibilities beyond the nature of man, such as sailing, flying, communicating by telephone, etc.

We may regard security as one of man's effort-saving devices. Precaution, anxiety, dread, which rise from insecurity, are forms of effort, an answer, as it were, to nature's imposition upon man.

Technology, then, is the means by which we shun, entirely or in part, the "things to do" which would have kept us busy under natural circumstances. This is generally agreed upon; but, oddly enough, technology has been looked at from one side only, from its obverse, so to speak, which is less interesting, while few people have been aware of the enigma upon its reverse.

Is it not puzzling that man should make an effort to save effort? One may say that technology is a small effort to save a very much larger one and therefore perfectly justified and reasonable. Good; but there is another question. What becomes of the saved energy? Does it just lie idle? What is man to do after he has eliminated what nature compels him to do? What fills his life? For doing nothing means to empty life, to not-live; it is incompatible with the constitution of man. The question, far from being fantastic, has grown very real during these last years. There are countries where the worker labors eight hours a day for five days a week, and under normal circumstances we might have had by now a four-day week. What is the worker to do with all that empty time on his hands?

The fact that our present technology discloses this problem so very clearly does not mean that it has not been present in all technologies at all times. They all entail a reduction of man's elemental activities and that not incidentally, as a by-product, but because the desire to save effort is the moving power behind them. This is no minor point; it concerns the very essence of technology which we have not understood rightly until we have found out where the free energy goes.

In the midst of our dissertation on technology we come upon the mystery of man's being as upon the core of a fruit. For he is an entity compelled, if he wants to live, to live in nature; he is an animal. Life in the zoological sense consists of such actions as are necessary for existence in nature. But man arranges things so that the claims of this life are reduced to a minimum. In the vacuum arising after he has left behind his animal life he devotes himself to a series of nonbiological occupations which are not imposed by nature but invented by himself. This invented life—invented as a novel or a play is invented—man calls "human life," well-being. Human life transcends the reality of nature. It is not given to man as its fall is given to a stone or the stock of its organic acts—eating, flying, nesting—to an animal. He makes it himself, beginning by inventing it. Have we heard right? Is human life in its most human dimension a work of fiction? Is man a sort of novelist of himself who conceives the fanciful figure of a personage with its unreal occupations and then, for the sake of converting it into reality, does all the things he does—and becomes an engineer?

IV EXCURSION TO THE SUBSTRUCTURE
OF TECHNOLOGY

The answers which have been given to the question, what is technology, are appallingly superficial; and what is worse, this cannot be blamed on chance. For the same happens to all questions dealing with what is truly human in human beings. There is no way of throwing light upon them until they are tackled in those profound strata from which everything properly human evolves. As long as we continue to speak of the problems that concern man as though we knew what man really is, we shall only succeed in invariably leaving the true issue behind. That is what happens with technology. We must realize into what fundamental depths our argument will lead us. How does it come to pass that there exists in the universe this strange thing called technology, the absolute cosmic fact of man the technician? If we seriously intend to find an answer, we must be ready to plunge into certain unavoidable profundities.

We shall then come upon the fact that an entity in the universe, man, has no other way of existing than by being in another entity, nature or the world. This relation of being one in the other, man in nature, might take on one of three possible aspects. Nature might offer man nothing but facilities for his existence in it. That would mean that the being of man coincides fully with that of nature or, what is the same, that man is a natural being. That is the case of the stone, the plant, and, probably, the animal. If it were that of man, too, he would be without necessities, he would lack nothing, he would not be needy. His desires and their satisfaction would be one and the same. He would wish for nothing that did not exist in the world and, conversely, whatever he wished for would be there of itself, as in the fairy tale of the magic wand. Such an entity could not experience the world as something alien to himself; for the world would offer him no resistance. He would be in the world as though he were in himself.

Or the opposite might happen. The world might offer to

man nothing but difficulties, i. e., the being of the world and the being of man might be completely antagonistic. In this case the world would be no abode for man; he could not exist in it, not even for the fraction of a second. There would be no human life and, consequently, no technology.

The third possibility is the one that prevails in reality. Living in the world, man finds that the world surrounds him as an intricate net woven of both facilities and difficulties. Indeed, there are not many things in it which, potentially, are not both. The earth supports him, enabling him to lie down when he is tired and to run when he has to flee. A shipwreck will bring home to him the advantage of the firm earth—a thing grown humble from habitude. But the earth also means distance. Much earth may separate him from the spring when he is thirsty. Or the earth may tower above him as a steep slope that is hard to climb. This fundamental phenomenon —perhaps the most fundamental of all—that we are surrounded by both facilities and difficulties gives to the reality called human life its peculiar ontological character.

For if man encountered no facilities it would be impossible for him to be in the world, he would not exist, and there would be no problem. Since he finds facilities to rely on, his existence is possible. But this possibility, since he also finds difficulties, is continually challenged, disturbed, imperiled. Hence, man's existence is no passive being in the world; it is an unending struggle to accommodate himself in it. The stone is given its existence; it need not fight for being what it is—a stone in the field. Man has to be himself in spite of unfavorable circumstances; that means he has to make his own existence at every single moment. He is given the abstract possibility of existing, but not the reality. This he has to conquer hour after hour. Man must earn his life, not only economically but metaphysically.

And all this for what reason? Obviously—but this is repeating the same thing in other words—because man's being and nature's being do not fully coincide. Because man's being is made of such strange stuff as to be partly akin to nature and partly not, at once natural and extranatural, a kind of ontological centaur, half immersed in nature, half transcending it. Dante would have likened him to a boat drawn up on the beach with one end of its keel in the water and the other in the sand. What is natural in him is realized by itself; it presents no problem. That is precisely why man does not consider it his true being. His extranatural part, on the other hand, is not there from the outset and of itself; it is but an aspiration, a project of life. And this we feel to be our true being; we call it our personality, our self. Our extra- and antinatural portion, however, must not be interpreted in terms of any of the older spiritual philosophies. I am not interested now in the so-called spirit (*Geist*), a pretty confused idea laden with speculative wizardry.

If the reader reflects a little upon the meaning of the entity he calls his life, he will find that it is the attempt to carry out a definite program or project of existence. And his self—each man's self—is nothing but this devised program. All we do we do in the service of this program. Thus man begins by being something that has no reality, neither corporeal nor spiritual; he is a project as such, something which is not yet but aspires to be. One may object that there can be no program without somebody having it, without an idea, a mind, a soul, or whatever it is called. I cannot discuss this thoroughly because it would mean embarking on a course of philosophy. But I will say this: although the project of being a great financier has to be conceived of in an idea, "being" the project is different from holding the idea. In fact, I find no difficulty in thinking this idea but I am very far from being this project.

Here we come upon the formidable and unparalleled character which makes man unique in the universe. We are dealing—and let the disquieting strangeness of the case be well noted—with an entity whose being consists not in what it is already, but in what it is not yet, a being that consists in not-yet-being. Everything else in the world

is what it is. An entity whose mode of being consists
what it is already, whose potentiality coincides at one
with his reality, we call a "thing." Things are given their
being ready-made.

In this sense man is not a thing but an aspiration, the
aspiration to be this or that. Each epoch, each nation, each
individual varies in its own way the general human aspiration.

Now, I hope, all terms of the absolute phenomenon
called "my life" will be clearly understood. Existence
means, for each of us, the process of realizing, under
given conditions, the aspiration we are. We cannot choose
the world in which to live. We find ourselves, without our
previous consent, embedded in an environment, a here
and now. And my environment is made up not only by
heaven and earth around me, but by my own body and my
own soul. I am not my body; I find myself with it, and
with it I must live, be it handsome or ugly, weak or
sturdy. Neither am I my soul; I find myself with it and
must use it for the purpose of living although it may lack
will power or memory and not be of much good. Body
and soul are things; but I am a drama, if anything, an
unending struggle to be what I have to be. The aspiration
or program I am, impresses its peculiar profile on the
world about me, and that world reacts to this impress,
accepting or resisting it. My aspiration meets with

hindrance or with furtherance in my environment.

At this point one remark must be made which would have been misunderstood before. What we call nature, circumstance, or the world is essentially nothing but a conjunction of favorable and adverse conditions encountered by man in the pursuit of this program. The three names are interpretations of ours; what we first come upon is the experience of being hampered or favored in living. We are wont to conceive of nature and world as existing by themselves, independent of man. The concept "thing" likewise refers to something that has a hard and fast being and has it by itself and apart from man. But I repeat, this is the result of an interpretative reaction of our intellect upon what first confronts us. What first confronts us has no being apart from and independent of us; it consists exclusively in presenting facilities and difficulties, that is to say, in what it is in respect to our aspiration. Only in relation to our vital program is something an obstacle or an aid. And according to the aspiration animating us the facilities and difficulties, making up our pure and fundamental environment, will be such or such, greater or smaller.

This explains why to each epoch and even to each individual the world looks different. To the particular profile of our personal project, circumstance answers with another definite profile of facilities and difficulties. The world of the businessman obviously is different from the world of the poet. Where one comes to grief, the other thrives; where one rejoices, the other frets. The two worlds, no doubt, have many elements in common, viz., those which correspond to the generic aspiration of man as a species. But the human species is incomparably less stable and more mutable than any animal species. Men have an intractable way of being enormously unequal in spite of all assurances to the contrary.

V LIFE AS AUTOFABRICATION—TECHNOLOGY
AND DESIRES

From this point of view human life, the existence of man, appears essentially problematic. To all other entities of the universe existence presents no problem. For existence means actual realization of an essence. It means, for instance, that "being a bull" actually occurs. A bull, if he exists, exists as a bull. For a man, on the contrary, to exist does not mean to exist at once as the man he is, but merely that there exists a possibility of, and an effort towards, accomplishing this. Who of us is all he should be and all he longs to be? In contrast to the rest of creation, man, in existing, has to make his existence. He has to solve the practical problem of transferring into reality the program that is himself. For this reason "my life" is pure task, a thing inexorably to be made. It is not given to me as a present; I have to make it. Life gives me much to do; nay, it is nothing save the "to do" it has in store for me. And this "to do" is not a thing, but action in the most active sense of the word.

In the case of other beings the assumption is that somebody or something, already existing, acts; here we are dealing with an entity that has to act in order to be; its being presupposes action. Man, willy-nilly, is self-made, autofabricated. The word is not unfitting. It emphasizes the fact that in the very root of his essence man finds himself called upon to be an engineer. Life means to him at once and primarily the effort to bring into existence what does not exist offhand, to wit: himself. In short, human life "is" production. By this I mean to say that fundamentally life is not, as has been believed for so many centuries, contemplation, thinking, theory, but action. It is fabrication; and it is thinking, theory, science only because these are needed for its autofabrication, hence secondarily, not primarily. To live . . . that is to find means and ways for realizing the program we are.

The world, the environment, presents itself as *materia prima* and possible machine for this purpose. Since man, in order to exist, has to be in the world and the world does not admit forthwith of the full realization of his being, he sets out to search around for the hidden instrument that may serve his ends. The history of human thinking may be regarded as a long series of observations made to discover what latent possibilities the world offers for the construction of machines. And it is not by chance, as we shall shortly see, that technology properly speaking, technology in the fullness of its maturity, begins around 1600, when man in the course of his theoretical thinking about the world comes to regard it as a machine. Modern technology is linked with the work of Galileo, Descartes, Huygens, i. e., with the mechanical interpretation of the universe. Before that, the corporeal world had been generally believed to be an a-mechanical entity, the ultimate essence of which was constituted by spiritual powers of more or less arbitrary and uncontrollable nature; whereas the world as pure mechanism is the machine of machines.

It is, therefore, a fundamental error to believe that man is an animal endowed with a talent for technology, in other words, that an animal might be transmuted into a man by magically grafting on it the technical gift. The opposite holds: because man has to accomplish a task fundamentally different from that of the animal, an extra-natural task, he cannot spend his energies in satisfying his elemental needs, but must stint them in this realm so as to be able to employ them freely in the odd pursuit of realizing his being in the world.

We now see why man begins where technology begins. The magic circle of leisure which technology opens up for him in nature is the cell where he can house his extra-natural being. This is why I have previously emphasized that the meaning and the final cause of technology lie outside itself, namely in the use man makes of the unoccupied energies it sets free. The mission of technology consists in releasing man for the task of being himself.

The ancients divided life into two spheres. The first they called *otium*, leisure, by which they understood not the negative of doing, not idling, but the positive attitude of seeing to the strictly human obligations of man, such as command, organization, social intercourse, science, arts. The second, consisting of those efforts which meet the elemental necessities and make *otium* possible, they called *nec-otium*, with apposite stress on the negative character it has for man.

Instead of living haphazardly and squandering his efforts, man must act according to a plan which helps him to obtain security in his clash with natural exigencies and to dominate them to his best advantage. This is the technical activity of man in contrast to the animal's life *au bon de Dieu*.

The particular human activities which deserve and have received the name of technology are only concrete specializations of the general character of the autofabrication inherent in human life. Were man not from the start compelled to construct, with the material of nature, the extranatural aspiration that he is, none of the technical arts would exist. The absolute fact called technology rises only from this strange, dramatic metaphysical occurrence, that two disparate entities—man and the world —find themselves under the obligation to coexist in such a way that one of them, man, has to install his extraworldly being in the other, which precisely is the world. The problem of how to do this, which indeed calls for an engineer, is the subject matter of human existence.

In spite of this, or rather because of it, technology is, strictly speaking, not the beginning of things. It will mobilize its ingenuity and perform the task life is; it will —within certain limits, of course—succeed in realizing the human project. But it does not draw up that project; the final aims it has to pursue come from elsewhere. The vital program is pretechnical. Man's technical capacity —that is, the technician—is in charge of inventing the simplest and safest way to meet man's necessities. But these, as we have seen, are in their turn inventions. They are what man in each epoch, nation, or individual aspires to be. Hence there exists a first, pretechnical invention par excellence, the original desire.

Now, desiring is by no means easy. The reader need only remember the particular quandary of the newly rich man. With all wish-fulfilling means at his command he finds himself in the awkward situation of not knowing how to wish. At the bottom of his heart he is aware that he wishes nothing, that he himself is unable to direct his appetite and to choose among the innumerable things offered by his environment. He has to look for a middleman to orient him. And he finds one in the predominant wishes of other people, whom he will entrust with wishing for him. Consequently, the first purchases of the newly rich are an automobile, a radio, and an electric shaver. As there are hackneyed thoughts, ideas which the man who thinks them has not thought originally and for himself but repeated blindly and automatically, so there are hackneyed wishes which are but the fiction and the gesture of genuine desire.

If this happens in the realm of wishing with objects which are there and lie to hand before they are wished for, one may imagine how difficult the properly creative wish must be, the wish that reaches out for things yet nonexistent and anticipates the still unreal. Every wish for this or that particular thing is ultimately connected with the person a man wants to be. This person, therefore, is the fundamental wish and the source of all other wishes. If a man is unable to wish for his own self because he has no clear vision of a self to be realized, he can have but pseudo wishes and spectral desires devoid of sincerity and vigor.

It may well be that one of the basic diseases of our

time is a crisis of wishing and that for this reason all our fabulous technical achievements seem to be of no use whatever. This now begins to dawn upon us all; but as far back as 1921 I happened to remark in my book *Invertebrate Spain* that "Europe is suffering from an exhaustion of her wishing power." When the vital program grows dim and hazy, technology, not knowing whom and what purpose to serve, is threatened with a setback.

For this is the absurd situation at which we have arrived: the wealth of material means that present-day man can count on for his living surpasses by far that of all other ages and we are clearly aware of its superabundance. Yet we suffer from an appalling restlessness because we do not know what to do with it, because we lack imagination for inventing our lives.

Why this? Well asked; but the question is not pertinent to our essay. Let us for all answer pose one in return: which part of man is it, or rather what sort of men are they, that are in special charge of the vital program? Poets, philosophers, politicians, founders of religions, discoverers of new values? We shall not venture on an answer but only state that the engineer is dependent on them all. Which explains why they all rank higher than he, a difference which has always existed and against which it would be in vain to protest.

This may have something to do with the curious fact

that technical achievements are more or less anonymous or, at least, that the glory which generally falls to great men of the former types is rarely enjoyed by technical inventors. Among the most important inventions of the last sixty years is the combustion engine. Who outside the ranks of professional engineers remembers offhand the illustrious names of its inventors?

For the same reason it is utterly improbable that a technocracy will ever be established. By the very definition of him, the engineer cannot take the helm, he cannot rule. His role is magnificent, highly admirable, but irremediably secondary.

To sum up, the reform of nature—or technology—is like all change a movement with two terms: a whence and a whither. The whence is nature, such as it is given. If nature is to be modified, the other term to which it has to conform must be fixed. The whither is man's program of life. What is the word for the fullness of its realization? Obviously well-being, happiness. And thus we have looped the loop of our argument.

VI MAN'S EXTRANATURAL DESTINY—THE ORIGIN
OF THE TIBETAN STATE—DIFFERENT
PROGRAMS OF BEING

When we said that technology is the system of activities through which man endeavors to realize the extranatural

program that is himself, we may have sounded somewhat cryptic and abstract. It may be helpful to enumerate
briefly some of the vital projects realized by man in the
course of history. There is the Hindu *bodhisattva;* the
athletic youth of the Greek aristocracy of the sixth century; the upright citizen of the Roman Republic and the
Stoic of the Empire; the medieval saint; the *hidalgo*
of the sixteenth century; the *homme de bonne compagnie*
of the *dix-septième;* the German *schöne Seele* of the end
of the eighteenth and the *Dichter und Denker* of the beginning of the nineteenth; the English gentleman of 1850,
etc.

But I must not allow myself to be lured into the fascinating task of describing the various profiles of the
world that correspond to these human modes of being. I
will point out only one fact which to me seems beyond
all doubt. A nation where the existence of the *bodhisattva* is regarded as man's true being cannot develop the
same technology as one in which people want to be gentlemen. The *bodhisattva* holds that true existence cannot
come to pass in this world of mere appearances where
man lives as an individual, an isolated part of the universe, but only when he has dissolved into the Whole and
disappeared in it. Not to live or to live as little as possible
is therefore the prime concern of the *bodhisattva*. He will
reduce his food to a minimum—bad for the food indus-

tries! He will remain as motionless as possible, absorbed
in meditation, the one vehicle by which he hopes to be
transported into a state of ecstasy and to come to live outside this world. Not much chance of his inventing the
automobile!

Instead, he will develop all those mental techniques
which seem so uncanny to Western minds, the techniques
of the fakir and the yogi, of ecstasy, insensibility, cata-
lepsy, concentration which bring about changes not in
the material world but in man's body and soul. This instance will make clear, I hope, why technology is a function of the variable program of man. It also throws some
light on the fact we have mentioned above, but not yet
fully understood, that man has an extranatural being.

A life of meditation and ecstasy, lived as though it
were not lived, in continuous endeavor to annul the world
and existence itself, cannot be called a natural life. To
be *bodhisattva* means in principle not to move, not to be
sexed, not to feel joy or pain; in one word, to be the living
negation of nature. It is indeed a drastic example of the
extranaturalness of human life and of the difficulty of its
realization in the world. A certain preparedness, a pre-
accommodation of the world seems indispensable if it is to
house at all an entity so radically at variance with it. A
scientist, bent on giving a naturalistic explanation to all
things human, is likely to jump at this remark, declaring

that such preparedness of nature is the main thing and that we were absolutely wrong in maintaining that man's project of life calls forth technology which in turn shapes nature so that it conforms to the human purpose. In India, he will say, by way of example, climate and soil facilitate human life to such a degree that there is hardly any need for man to move and to eat. Thus, climate and soil are conducive to the Buddhistic type of life. This, I expect, is the first time that something in my essay appeals to the scientists among my readers, if such there be.

But now I cannot help spoiling even this small satisfaction for them. No; there doubtless exists a relation between climate and soil on the one hand and man's program on the other, but it is very different from what their explanation supposes. I will not describe here what it really is. For once I should like to be excused from reasoning and be allowed simply to contrast with the fact adduced by my presumed opponent another fact that bears witness against his explanation.

If the climate and the soil of India are responsible for Buddhism in India, why then should Tibet now be the foremost land of Buddhism? Its climate and soil contrast markedly with those of the Ganges and Ceylon. The high tableland behind the Himalayas is among the most inhospitable and inclement regions of the globe. Fierce storms sweep over those immense plains and wide valleys. Blizzards and frosts haunt them for the best part of the year. The original inhabitants were rugged, roving hordes in continuous feud with one another. They lived in tents made of the hides of the great sheep of the table-land. No state could ever establish itself in those regions.

But one day Buddhistic missionaries climbed over the grisly Himalayan passes and converted some of these hordes to their religion. Now, Buddhism is more than any other religion a matter of meditation. It knows of no god who takes upon his own shoulders the salvation of man. Man has to see to it himself by means of meditation and prayer. But how meditate in the grim Tibetan climate? The answer was the construction of monasteries of stone and stucco, the first buildings ever seen in that part of the world. In Tibet, therefore, the house came into being for man to pray in, not to live in. But now it happened that in the customary tribal campaigns the Buddhist hordes took shelter in their houses, which thus acquired a military significance, furnishing their owners with a certain superiority over the non-Buddhists. To make a long story short: the monastery functioning as a fortress created the Tibetan State. Here Buddhism does not spring from the climate and the soil but, on the contrary, Buddhism as a "human necessity," that is to say, something life is able to do without, through the art of building, modifies the climate and the soil with respect to their influence on social and political circumstances.

This, by the way, also furnishes a good example of the solidarity between the different technical arts. It shows how easy an artifact invented to serve one purpose may be used for others. We have already seen that the primitive bow, which most probably originated as a musical instrument, became a weapon for war and the hunt. An analogous case is presented by the story of Tyrtaeus, that ridiculous general lent by the Athenians to the Spartans in the second Messenian war. Old, lame, and the author of outmoded elegies to boot, he was the laughingstock of the *jeunesse dorée* in Attica. But lo and behold, he comes to Sparta and the demoralized Lacedaemonians begin winning all the battles. Why? For a technical reason of tactics. Tyrtaeus's elegies, composed in a clearly accentuated archaic rhythm, lend themselves beautifully to marching songs and make for a stricter unity of movement in the Spartan phalanx. Thus a technical item of the art of poetry turned out to be important in the art of warfare.

But enough of digressions. We were bent on contrasting the two situations of man that ensue from his aspiration to be a gentleman or a *bodhisattva*. The difference is radical. It will become quite clear when we point out some characteristics of the gentleman. Concerning the gentleman we must first state that he is not the same as an aristocrat. No doubt, English aristocrats were the first to invent this mode of being, but they were actuated by those tendencies which have always distinguished the English noblemen from all other types of noblemen. While the others were hermetic as a class and likewise hermetic regarding the type of occupations they deigned to devote themselves to—war, politics, diplomacy, sport, agriculture on a large scale—since the sixteenth century the English aristocrat held his own in commerce, industry, and the liberal professions. As history from that time on has mainly consisted in activities of this sort he has been the only aristocrat to survive in full social efficiency. This made it possible for England to create in the beginning of the nineteenth century a prototype of existence which was to become exemplary throughout the world. Members of the middle class and the working class can, to a certain degree, be gentlemen. Nay more, whatever happens in a future which, alas, may be imminent there will remain as one of the miracles of history the fact that today even the humblest English workman is in his sphere a gentleman. Gentlemanliness does not imply nobility. The continental aristocrat of the last four centuries is, primarily, an heir—a man who has

large means of living at his command without having
had to earn them. The gentleman as such is not an heir.
On the contrary, the supposition is that a man has to
earn his living and to have an occupation, preferably
a practical one—the gentleman is no intellectual—and
it is precisely in his profession that he has to behave as
a gentleman. Antipodes of the gentleman are the *gentil-
homme* of Versailles and the Prussian *Junker*.

VII THE GENTLEMAN TYPE—ITS TECHNICAL
REQUIREMENTS—THE GENTLEMAN
AND THE *HIDALGO*

But what does it mean to be a gentleman? Let us take
a short cut and, exaggerating things, put it this way: a
gentleman is a man who displays throughout his life,
i. e., in every situation however serious or unpleasant, a
type of behavior which customarily remains restricted to
those brief moments when the pressures and responsibilities of life are shuffled off and man indulges in the
diversion of a game. This again shows strikingly to
what degree the human program of life can be extra-
natural. For games and their rules are sheer invention
in comparison with life as it comes from nature's own
hands. The gentleman ideal inverts the terms within
human life itself, proposing that a man should behave in

his enforced existence of struggle with his environment as though he moved in the unreal and purely imaginative orbit of his games and sports.

When people are in the mood to play we may assume that they feel comparatively safe regarding the elemental needs of life. Games are a luxury not to be indulged in before the lower zones of existence are well taken care of, and an abundance of means guarantees a life within an ample margin of serene tranquillity, unharassed by the stress and strain of penury which converts everything into a frightening problem. In this state of mind man delights in his own magnanimity and gratifies himself with playing fair. He will defend his cause but without ceasing to respect the other fellow's rights. He will not cheat, for cheating means to give up the attitude of play: it is "not cricket." The game, it is true, is an effort, but an effort which is at rest in itself, free from the uneasiness that hovers about every kind of compulsory work because such work must be accomplished at all costs.

This explains the manners of the gentleman, his sense of justice, his veracity, his perfect self-control based on previous control of his surroundings, his clear awareness of his personal claims on others and theirs on him, viz., his duties. He would not think of using trickery. What is done must be done well, and that is all there is to it. English industrial products are known to be good and solid both in raw material and in workmanship. They are not made to be sold at any price. They are the opposite of trash. The English manufacturer has never condescended to conform to the taste and caprices of his customer as has the German. On the contrary, he calmly expects his customer to conform to his products. He does but little advertising which is always deceit, rhetoric, foul play. And the same in politics. No phrases, no farces, no demagogic inveiglement, no intolerance, but few laws; for the law, once it is written, turns into a reign of pure words which, since words cannot be fulfilled to the letter, necessarily results in falsification of the law and governmental dishonesty. A nation of gentlemen needs no constitution. Therefore England has fared very well without it. And so forth.

The gentleman, in contrast to the *bodhisattva*, wants to live intensely in this world and to be as much of an individual as he possibly can, centered in himself and filled with a sense of independence of everything else. In Paradise, where existence itself is a delightful game, the gentleman would be incongruous, the gentleman's concern being precisely to remain a good sport in the thick of rude reality. The principal element, the atmosphere, as it were, of the gentlemanly existence is a basic feeling of leisure derived from an ample control over the world. In stifling surroundings one cannot hope to breed gentlemen. This type of man, bent on converting existence into a game and a sport, is therefore very far from being an illusionist. He acts as he does just because he knows life to be hard, serious, and difficult. And just because he knows this he is anxious to secure control over circumstance—matter and man. That is how the British grew to be great engineers and great politicians.

The desire of the gentleman to be an individual and to give to his mundane destiny the grace of a game made it necessary for him to live remote from people and things, even physically, and to ennoble the humblest functions of his body by attending to them with elaborate care. The details of personal cleanliness, the ceremony of dressing for dinner, the daily bath—after Roman times there were hardly any private baths in the Western world—are punctiliously observed. I apologize for mentioning that England gave us the w.c. A dyed-in-the-wool intellectual would never have thought of inventing it, for he despises his body. But the gentleman, as we have said, is no intellectual; and so he is concerned about decorum: clean body, clean soul.

All this, of course, is based on wealth. The gentleman ideal both presupposed and produced large fortunes. Its virtues cannot unfold without an ample margin of economic power. As a matter of fact, the gentleman type reached its perfection only in the middle of the last century when England had become fabulously rich. The English worker can, in his way, be a gentleman because he earns more than the average member of the middle class in other countries.

It would be of no small interest if someone with a good mind and a long intimate knowledge of the English situation were to study the present state of the system of vital norms which we have called the gentleman ideal. During the last twenty years economic circumstances in England have changed. She is much less rich than in the beginning of this century. Can one be poor and still be English? Can the characteristic English virtues survive in an atmosphere of scarcity?

Be that as it may, it is not unfitting to think of an exemplary type of life that preserves the best qualities of the gentleman and yet is compatible with the impoverishment that inexorably threatens our planet. If we try to visualize this new figure, there will inevitably rise before our mind's eye as a term of comparison another human profile evolved in history, which in some of its features bears close resemblance to the portrait of the gentleman while differing from it in one respect: it thrives on the soil of poverty. I mean the Spanish *hidalgo*. In contrast to the gentleman the *hidalgo* does not work. He reduces his material necessities to a minimum and consequently has no use for technology. He lives in poverty, it is true, like those plants of the desert which have learned to grow without moisture. But it is also beyond question that he knows how to lend dignity to his wretched conditions. Dignity makes him the equal of his more fortunate brother, the gentleman.

VIII THINGS AND THEIR "BEING"—THE PRE-THING —MAN, ANIMALS, TOOLS—EVOLUTION OF TECHNOLOGY

After this digression into a few concrete examples, we now take up again the main trend of our investigation. I have been anxious to stress those assumptions and implications of the phenomenon of technology which, though they really are its essence, usually remain unobserved. For a thing is above all the series of conditions which make it possible. Kant would have called them "conditions of possibility" and Leibnitz in his clearer and soberer way "ingredients" or "requisites."

But now I am certain there will be objections from my readers. Among them, I fear, are quite a few who listen only because they hope to hear what they know already in more or less distinct details and not because they have decided to open their minds to what I have to say—the more unexpected the better. These, I fear, will have thought to themselves: now, what can all this have to do with technology, I mean real technology, the way it works?

They are unaware that if we want to answer the question, what is this thing, we must break up the form in which it exists and functions here before our eyes and try to isolate it and to describe its ingredients. None of these, it is evident, is the thing; the thing is their result. If we want to restore the thing, its ingredients as such and in their isolation must disappear for us. We can see water only after we have ceased to see oxygen and hydrogen. A thing is defined through an enumeration of its ingredients; and its ingredients, its presuppositions, its implications, become therefore something like a pre-thing. It is this essence of the thing, this pre-thing, which must be brought to light; for the thing is there already and need not be discovered. In return, the pre-thing shows the thing in *statu nascendi;* and we do not really know a thing unless we have, in one sense or another, been present at its birth.

The "requisites" or "ingredients" of technology we have thus far pointed out are certainly not all, but they are the deepest and therefore the most easily overlooked, whereas we may be sure no one will fail to see that man would never have invented tools to satisfy his necessities had not his intelligence enabled him to discover new relations between the things about him. This seems obvious; and yet it is not conclusive. Being able to do something is no sufficient reason for doing it. The fact that man possesses technical intelligence does not necessarily entail the existence of technology; for technical intelligence is an ability, but technology is actual performance which may or may not take place. And we are interested here not in finding out whether man is endowed with technical ability, but in understanding why such a thing as technology exists. This, however, will become intelligible only after the discovery that man has to be an engineer, no matter whether he is gifted for it or not.

It may seem obvious to hold intelligence responsible for both the existence of technology and the difference between man and animals. But we should by this time have lost the calm belief with which, two centuries ago, Benjamin Franklin could still define man as the "tool-making animal." Mr. Koehler's famous experiments with chimpanzees as well as observations in other fields of animal psychology have revealed that animals possess a certain ability for manufacturing tools. If they are not able of taking full advantage of tools, it is owing not to lack of intelligence, strictly speaking, but to other peculiarities of their constitution. Mr. Koehler shows that the essential deficiency of the chimpanzee is its memory. Because it will forget what has happened to it only a minute ago, its intelligence finds but scanty material for creative combinations.

What distinguishes man from animals is not so much the difference of their psychic mechanisms in themselves as the consequences which arise from this difference and give completely dissimilar structures to their respective existences. The animal has not enough imagination to draw up a project of life other than the mere monotonous repetition of its previous actions. And this is enough to bring about an absolutely different reality of life in the two cases. If life is not realization of a program, intelligence becomes a purely mechanical function without discipline and orientation. One forgets too easily that intelligence, however keen, cannot furnish its own direction and therefore is unable to attain to actual technical discoveries. It does not know by itself what to prefer among the countless "inventable" things and is lost in their unlimited possibilities. Technical capacity can arise only in an entity whose intelligence functions in the service of an imagination pregnant not with technical, but with vital projects.

One of the purposes of the foregoing argument has been to warn against the spontaneous but injudicious tendency of our time to believe that, at bottom, no more than one technology exists, the present America-European technology, and that all others are but awkward stammerings, rudimentary attempts. I have opposed this tendency and embedded our present technology, as one among many others, in the vast and multiform panorama of human technology in its entirety, thereby relativizing its meaning and showing that every way and project of life has its corresponding specific form of technology.

But now that this is done, I must proceed to describe the characteristics of modern technology and to point out in particular why it has appeared to us, with some semblance of truth after all, as the technology par excellence. In fact, technology has for many reasons attained today among the integral components of human life a position which it has never held before. True, it has been in all times important enough; witness the historian who, when he tries to find a common denominator for vast periods of prehistoric time, resorts to the peculiarities of their technologies, calling the primeval age of humanity—which we faintly discern as though by the light of early dawn—the eolithic or auroral stone age and going on with the paleolithic or early stone age, the bronze age, and so forth. Yet on this list our own time would have to figure not as the age of this or that technology, but simply as the age of technology. How could the evolution of man's technical capacity bring forth an epoch in which we can adequately characterize man, who, after all, has always been an engineer, by defining him merely as such? It is evident that this could occur only because the relation between man and technology had been raised to an extraordinarily high power; and this rise must in its turn have been produced by a radical modification in the technical function itself.

Insight into the specific character of modern technology itself will best be gained by deliberately setting off its peculiar silhouette against the background of the whole of man's technical past. This means that we must give a sketch, if only the briefest, of the great changes undergone by the technical function itself; in other words, that we must define various stages in the evolution of technology. In this way, drawing some border lines and underlining others, we shall see the hazy past take on relief and perspective, revealing the forms from which technology has set out and those to which it has been coming.

IX THE STAGES OF TECHNOLOGY— TECHNOLOGY OF CHANCE

The subject is difficult. It took me some time to decide upon the principle best suited to distinguish periods of technology. I do not hesitate to reject the one readiest to hand, viz., that we should divide the evolution according to the appearance of certain momentous and characteristic inventions. All I have said in this essay aims to correct the current error of regarding such or such a definite invention as the thing which matters in technology. What really matters and what can bring about a fundamental advance is a change in the general character of technology. No single invention is of such caliber as to bear comparison with the tremendous mass of the integral evolution. We have seen that magnificent advances have been achieved only to be lost again, whether they disappeared completely or whether they had to be rediscovered.

Nay more, an invention may be made sometime and somewhere and still fail to take on its true technical significance. Gunpowder and the printing press, unquestionably two discoveries of great pith and moment, were known in China for centuries without being of much use. It is not before the fifteenth century in Europe that gunpowder and the printing press, the former probably in Lombardy, the latter in Germany, became historical powers. With this in view, when shall we say they were invented? No doubt, they grew effective in history only when they appeared incorporated in the general body of late medieval technology, serving the purposes of the program of life operative in that age. Firearms and the printing press are contemporaries of the compass. They all bear the same marks, so characteristic, as we shall shortly see, of that hour between Gothic and Renaissance, the scientific endeavors of which culminated in Copernicus. The reader will observe that, each in its own manner, they establish contact between man and things at a distance from him. They belong to the instruments of the *actio in distans,* which is at the root of modern technology. The cannon brings distant armies into immediate touch with each other. The compass throws a bridge between man and the cardinal points. The printing press brings the solitary writer into the presence of the infinite orbit of possible readers.

The best principle of delimiting periods in technical evolution is, to my judgment, furnished by the relation between man and technology, in other words by the conception which man in the course of history held, not of this or that particular technology but of the technical function as such. In applying this principle we shall see that it not only clarifies the past, but also throws light on the question we have asked before: how could modern technology give birth to such radical changes, and why is the part it plays in human life unparalleled in any previous age?

Taking this principle as our point of departure we come to discern three main periods in the evolution of technology: technology of chance; technology of the craftsman; technology of the technician.

What I call technology of chance, because in it chance is the engineer responsible for the invention, is the primitive technology of pre- and protohistoric man and of the contemporary savage, viz., of the least-advanced groups of mankind—as the Vedas in Ceylon, the Semang in Borneo, the pigmies in New Guinea and Central Africa, the Australian Negroes, etc.

How does primitive man conceive technology? The answer is easy. He is not aware of his technology as such; he is unconscious of the fact that there is among his faculties one which enables him to refashion nature after his desires.

The repertory of technical acts at the command of primitive man is very small and does not form a body of sufficient volume to stand out against, and be distinguished from, that of his natural acts, which is incomparably more important. That is to say, primitive man is very little man and almost all animal. His technical acts are scattered over and merged into the totality of his natural acts and appear to him as part of his natural life. He finds himself with the ability to light a fire as he finds himself with the ability to walk, swim, use his arms . . . His natural acts are a given stock fixed once and for all; and so are his technical. It does not occur to him that technology is a means of virtually unlimited changes and advances.

The simplicity and scantiness of these pristine technical acts account for their being executed indiscriminately by all members of the community, who all light fires, carve bows and arrows, and so forth. The one differentiation noticeable very early is that women perform certain technical functions and men certain others. But that does not help primitive man to recognize technology as an isolated phenomenon. For the repertory of natural acts is also somewhat different in men and women. That the woman should plow the field—it was she who invented agriculture—appears as natural as that she should bear the children.

Nor does technology at this stage reveal its most characteristic aspect, that of invention. Primitive man is unaware that he has the power of invention; his inventions are not the result of a premeditated and deliberate search. He does not look for them; they seem rather to look for him. In the course of his constant and fortuitous manipulation of objects he may suddenly and by mere chance come upon a new useful device. While for fun or out of sheer restlessness he rubs two sticks together a spark springs up, and a vision of new connections between things will dawn upon him. The stick, which hitherto has served as weapon or support, acquires the new aspect of a thing producing fire. Our savage will be awed, feeling that nature has inadvertently loosed one of its secrets before him. Since fire had always seemed a godlike power, arousing religious emotions, the new fact is prone to take on a magic tinge. All primitive technology smacks of magic. In fact, magic, as we shall shortly see, is nothing but a kind of technology, albeit a frustrated and illusory one.

Primitive man does not look upon himself as the inventor of his inventions. Invention appears to him as another dimension of nature, as part of nature's power to furnish him—nature furnishing man, not man nature —with certain novel devices. He feels no more responsible for the production of his implements than for that of his hands and feet. He does not conceive of himself as *homo faber*. He is therefore very much in the same situation as Mr. Koehler's monkey when it suddenly notices that the stick in his hands may serve an unforeseen purpose. Mr. Koehler calls this the "aha-impression" after the exclamation of surprise a man utters when coming upon a startling new relation between things. It is obviously a case of the biological law of trial and error applied to the mental sphere. The infusoria "try" various movements and eventually find one with favorable effects on them which they consequently adopt as a function.

The inventions of primitive man, being, as we have

seen, products of pure chance, will obey the laws of probability. Given the number of possible independent combinations of things, a certain possibility exists of their presenting themselves some day in such an arrangement as to enable man to see preformed in them a future implement.

X TECHNOLOGY AS CRAFTSMANSHIP—TECHNOLOGY OF THE TECHNICIAN

We come to the second stage, the technology of the artisan. This is the technology of Greece, of preimperial Rome, and of the Middle Ages. Here are in swift enumeration some of its essential features.

The repertory of technical acts has grown considerably. But—and this is important—a crisis and setback, or even the sudden disappearence of the principal industrial arts, would not yet be a fatal blow to material life in these societies. The life people lead with all these technical comforts and the life they would have to lead without them are not so radically different as to bar, in case of failures or checks, retreat to a primitive or almost primitive existence. The proportion between the technical and the nontechnical is not yet such as to make the former indispensable for the supporting of life. Man is still relying mainly on nature. At least, and that is what matters, so he himself feels. When technical crises arise he does therefore not realize that they will hamper his life, and consequently fails to meet them in time and with sufficient energy.

Having made this reservation we may now state that technical acts have by this time enormously increased both in number and in complexity. It has become necessary for a definite group of people to take them up systematically and make a full-time job of them. These people are the artisans. Their existence is bound to help man become conscious of technology as an independent entity. He sees the craftsman at work—the cobbler, the blacksmith, the mason, the saddler—and therefore comes to think of technology in terms and in the guise of the technician, the artisan. That is to say, he does not yet know that there is technology, but he knows that there are technicians who perform a peculiar set of activities which are not natural and common to all men.

Socrates in his struggle, which is so appallingly modern, with the people of his time began by trying to convince them that technology is not the same as the technician, that it is an abstract entity of its own not to be mixed up with this or that concrete man who possesses it.

At the second stage of technology everybody knows shoemaking to be a skill peculiar to certain men. It can be greater or smaller and suffer slight variations as do natural skills, running for instance, or swimming or, better still, the flying of a bird, the charging of a bull. That means shoemaking is now recognized as exclusively human and not natural, i. e., animal; but it is still looked upon as a gift granted and fixed once and for all. Since it is something exclusively human it is extra-natural, but since it is something fixed and limited, a definite fund not admitting of substantial amplification, it partakes of nature; and thus technology belongs to the nature of man. As man finds himself equipped with the unexchangeable system of his bodily movements, so he finds himself equipped with the fixed system of the "arts." For this is the name technology bears in nations and epochs living on the technical level in question; and this also is the original meaning of the Greek word *techne*.

The way technology progresses might disclose that it is an independent and, in principle, unlimited function. But, oddly enough, this fact becomes even less apparent in this than in the primitive period. After all, the few primitive inventions, being so fundamental, must have stood out melodramatically against the workaday routine of animal habits. But in craftsmanship there is no room whatever for a sense of invention. The artisan must learn thoroughly in long apprenticeship—it is the time of masters and apprentices—elaborate usages handed down by long tradition. He is governed by the norm that man must bow to tradition as such. His mind is turned towards the past and closed to novel possibilities. He follows the established routine. Even such modifications and improvements as may be brought about in his craft through continuous and therefore imperceptible shifts present themselves not as fundamental novelties, but rather as differences of personal style and skill. And these styles of certain masters again will spread in the forms of schools and thus retain the outward character of tradition.

We must mention another decisive reason why the idea of technology is not at this time separated from the idea of the person who practices it. Invention has as yet produced only tools and not machines. The first machine in the strict sense of the word—and with it I anticipate the third period—was the weaving machine set up by Robert in 1825. It is the first machine because it is the first tool that works by itself, and by itself produces the object. Herewith technology ceases to be what it was before, handiwork, and becomes mechanical production. In the crafts the tool works as a complement of man; man with his natural actions continues to be the principal agent. In the machine the tool comes to the fore, and now it is no longer the machine that serves man but man who waits on the machine. Working by itself, emancipated from man, the machine, at this stage, finally reveals that technology is a function apart and highly independent of natural man, a function which reaches far beyond the bounds set for him. What a man can do with his fixed animal activities we know beforehand; his scope is limited. But what the machine man is capable of inventing may do, is in principle unlimited.

One more feature of craftsmanship remains to be mentioned which helps to conceal the true character of technology. I mean this: technology implies two things. First, the invention of a plan of activity, of a method or procedure—*mechane*, said the Greeks—and, secondly, the execution of this plan. The former is technology strictly speaking, the latter consists merely in handling the raw material. In short, we have the technician and the worker who between them, performing very different functions, discharge the technical job. The craftsman is both technician and worker; and what appears first is a man at work with his hands, and what appears last, if at all, is the technology behind him. The dissociation of the artisan into his two ingredients, the worker and the technician, is one of the principal symptoms of the technology of the third period.

We have anticipated some of the traits of this technology. We have called it the technology of the technician. Man becomes clearly aware that there is a capacity

in him which is totally different from the immutable
activities of his natural or animal part. He realizes that
technology is not a haphazard discovery, as in the primitive period; that it is not a given and limited skill of
some people, the artisans, as in the second period; that
it is not this or that definite and therefore fixed "art";
but that it is a source of practically unlimited human
activity.

This new insight into technology as such puts man in a
situation radically new in his whole history and in a
way contrary to all he has experienced before. Hitherto
he has been conscious mainly of all the things he is
unable to do, i. e., of his deficiencies and limitations.
But the conception our time holds of technology—let
the reader reflect a moment on his own—places us in
a really tragicomic situation. Whenever we imagine
some utterly extravagant feat, we catch ourselves in a
feeling almost of apprehension lest our reckless dream
—say a voyage to the stars—should come true. Who
knows but that tomorrow morning's paper will spring
upon us the news that it has been possible to send a
projectile to the moon by imparting to it a speed great
enough to overcome the gravitational attraction. That is to
say, present-day man is secretly frightened by his own
omnipotence. And this may be another reason why he

does not know what he is. For finding himself in principle capable of being almost anything makes it all the harder for him to know what he actually is.

In this connection I want to draw attention to a point which does not properly belong here, that technology for all its being a practically unlimited capacity will irretrievably empty the lives of those who are resolved to stake everything on their faith in it and it alone. To be an engineer and nothing but an engineer means to be potentially everything and actually nothing. Just because of its promise of unlimited possibilities technology is an empty form like the most formalistic logic and is unable to determine the content of life. That is why our time, being the most intensely technical, is also the emptiest in all human history.

XI RELATION BETWEEN MAN AND TECHNOLOGY
IN OUR TIME—THE ENGINEER IN ANTIQUITY

This third stage of technical evolution, which is our own, is characterized by the following features:

Technical acts and achievements have increased enormously. Whereas in the Middle Ages—the era of the artisan—technology and the nature of man counterbalanced each other and the conditions of life made it possible to benefit from the human gift of adapting nature to man without denaturalizing man, in our time the technical devices outweigh the natural ones so gravely that material life would be flatly impossible without them. This is no manner of speaking, it is the literal truth. In *The Revolt of the Masses* I drew attention to the most noteworthy fact that the population of Europe between 500 and 1800 A. D., i. e., for thirteen centuries, never exceeded 180 millions; whereas by now, in little over a century, it has reached 500 millions, not counting those who have emigrated to America. In one century it has grown nearly three and a half times its size. If today 500 million people can live well in a space where 180 lived badly before, it is evident that, whatever the minor causes, the immediate cause and most necessary condition is the perfection of technology. Were technology to suffer a setback, millions of people would perish.

Such fecundity of the human animal could occur only after man had succeeded in interposing between himself and nature a zone of exclusively technical provenance, solid and thick enough to form something like a supernature. Present-day man—I refer not to the individual but to the totality of men—has no choice of whether to live in nature or to take advantage of this supernature. He is as irremediably dependent on, and lodged in, the latter as primitive man is in his natural environment. And that entails certain dangers. Since present-day man, as soon as he opens his eyes to life, finds himself surrounded by a superabundance of technical objects and procedures forming an artificial environment of such compactness that primordial nature is hidden behind it, he will tend to believe that all these things are there in the same way as nature itself is there without further effort on his part: that aspirin and automobiles grow on trees like apples. That is to say, he may easily lose sight of technology and of the conditions—the moral conditions, for example—under which it is produced and return to the primitive attitude of taking it for the gift of nature which is simply there. We thus have the curious fact that, at first, the prodigious expansion of technology made it stand out against the sober background of man's natural activities and allowed him to gain full sight of it, whereas by now its fantastic progress threatens to obscure it again.

Another feature helping man to discover the true character of his own technology we found to be the transition from mere tools to machines, i. e., mechanically working apparatus. A modern factory is a self-sufficient establishment waited on occasionally by a few persons of very modest standing. In consequence, the technician and the worker, who were united in the artisan, have been separated and the technician has grown to be the live expression of technology as such—in a word, the engineer.

Today technology stands before our mind's eye for what it is, apart, unmistakable, isolated, and unobscured by elements other than itself. And this enables certain persons, called engineers, to devote their lives to it. In the paleolithic age or in the Middle Ages technology, that is invention, could not have been a profession because man was ignorant of his own inventive power. Today the engineer embraces as one of the most normal and firmly established forms of activity the occupation of inventor. In contrast to the savage, he knows before he begins to invent that he is capable of doing so, which means that he has "technology" before he has "a technology." To this degree and in this concrete sense our previous assertion holds that technologies are nothing but concrete realizations of the general technical function of man. The engineer need not wait for chances and favorable odds; he is sure to make discoveries. How can he be?

The question obliges us to say a word about the technique of technology. To some people technique and nothing else is technology. They are right in so far as without technique—the intellectual method operative in technical creation—there is no technology. But with technique alone there is none either. As we have seen before, the existence of a capacity is not enough to put that capacity into action.

I should have liked to talk at leisure and in detail about both present and past techniques of technology. It is perhaps the subject in which I myself am most interested. But it would have been a mistake to let our investigations gravitate entirely around it. Now that this essay is breathing its last I must be content to give the matter brief consideration—brief, yet, I hope, sufficiently clear.

No doubt, technology could not have expanded so gloriously in these last centuries, nor the machine have replaced the tool, nor the artisan have been split up into his components, the worker and the engineer, had not the method of technology undergone a profound transformation.

Our technical methods are radically different from those of all earlier technologies. How can we best explain the diversity? Perhaps through the following question: how would an engineer of the past, supposing he was a real engineer and his invention was not due to chance but deliberately searched for, go about his task? I will give a schematic and therefore exaggerated example which is, however, historical and not fictitious. The Egyptian architect who built the pyramid of Cheops

was confronted with the problem of lifting stone blocks
to the highest parts of the monument. Starting as he
needs must from the desired end, namely to lift the
stones, he looked around for devices to achieve this.
"This," I have said, meaning he is concerned with the
result as a whole. His mind is absorbed by the final aim
in its integrity. He will therefore consider as possible
means only such procedures as will bring about the
total result at once, in one operation that may take more
or less time but which is homogeneous in itself. The unbroken unity of the end prompts him to look for a similarly uniform and undifferentiated means. This ac-
counts for the fact that in the early days of technology
the instrument through which an aim is achieved tends
to resemble the aim itself. Thus in the construction of
the pyramid the stones are raised to the top over another
pyramid, an earthen pyramid with a wider base and a
more gradual slope, which abuts against the first. Since
a solution found through this principle of similitude—
similia similibus—is not likely to be applicable in many
cases, the engineer has no general rule and method to
lead him from the intended aim to the adequate means.
All he can do is to try out empirically such possibilities
as offer more or less hope of serving his purpose. Within
the circle defined by his special problem he thus falls
back into the attitude of the primitive inventor.

XII MODERN TECHNICAL METHODS—THE CLOCKS
OF CHARLES V—SCIENCE AND WORKSHOP
—THE MIRACLE OF OUR TIME

The sixteenth century saw the rise of a new way of thinking manifest in technology as well as in the science of physics. Nay more, it was an essential feature of this new way of thinking that it is impossible to tell where it began, whether in the solution of practical problems or in the construction of pure ideas. In both realms Leonardo da Vinci was the harbinger of the new age. He was at home not only and not even principally in the painter's studio, but also in the workshop of the mechanician. All his life he was busy inventing "gadgets."

In the letter in which he begged for employment in Ludovico Moro's services he enclosed a long list of war machines and hydraulic apparatus of his invention. As in the Hellenistic period the battles and sieges of the great Demetrius Poliorcetes brought about the progress of mechanics which was to culminate in Archimedes, so the wars of the end of the fifteenth and the beginning of the sixteenth century stimulated the development of the new technology. Be it observed, the Diadochian wars, as well as those of the Renaissance, were sham wars, not fierce wars between hostile nations; they were wars of the military against the military, cold-blooded wars of brains and cannons, not wars of fiery hearts: therefore, technical wars.

About 1540 "mechanics" was a fad. At that time the word did not yet signify the science we understand by it. It referred to machinery and the art of building it. This was the meaning it still held in 1600 for Galileo, the father of mechanics as a science. Everybody was eager for apparatus, large or small, useful or simply amusing. When the great Charles V, the black-armored victor of Mühlberg, retired to the monastery of Yuste in one of the most illustrious examples of life's decline recorded in history, he took with him on his sublime voyage into oblivion but two objects from the world he left behind: clocks and Juanelo Turriano. The latter was a Fleming, a real magician in mechanical inventions, the deviser not only of the aqueducts which supplied Toledo with water—part of their ruins are still to be seen— but also of the automatic bird that fluttered on metal wings through the vast emptiness of the room where Charles V rested far from the maddening crowd.

Due emphasis should be laid on the fact that the greatest miracle wrought by the human mind, the science of physics, originated in technology. The young Galileo worked not at a university, but in the arsenals of Venice among cranes and levers. It was there that his mind was shaped.

In fact, the new technology proceeds in exactly the same way as the *nuova scienza*. The engineer no longer passes directly from the image of the desired end to the search of the means which may obtain it. He stands before the envisaged aim and begins to work on it. He analyzes it. That is to say, he breaks down the total result into the components which have formed it, e. g., into its "causes."

This is the method applied to physics by Galileo, who is known to have been an eminent inventor to boot. An Aristotelian scientist would not have thought of splitting up a phenomenon into its elements. He tried to find for it in its totality a cause likewise total; for the drowsiness produced by poppy juice the *virtus dormitiva*. Galileo proceeded in the opposite way. When observing an object in motion he asked for the elementary and therefore general movements of which the concrete movement was made up. This is the new mode of thinking: analysis of nature.

The union between the new technology and the new science is one not of superficial resemblance but of identical intellectual method. Herein lies the source of the independence and self-sufficiency of modern technology. It is neither magical inspiration nor pure chance, but "method," a pre-established, systematic way of thinking, conscious of its own foundations.

What a lesson! The scholar, we learn, must long and patiently manipulate the objects of his investigation and be in close contact with them—the scientist with material, the historian with human things. Had the German historians of the nineteenth century been better politicians or even better men of the world, who knows but that history might by now be a science, and we might have at our command a really efficient method for handling the great collective phenomena before which, with shame be it said, present-day man finds himself adopting the same attitude as the paleolithic savage before lightning.

The so-called spirit is an all too ethereal agent, permanently in danger of being lost in the labyrinth of its own infinite possibilities. Thinking is too easy. The mind in its flight rarely meets with resistance. Hence the vital importance for the intellectual of touching concrete objects and of learning discipline in his intercourse with them. Bodies are the mentors of the spirit, as Chiron, the centaur, was the mentor of the Greek heroes. Without the check of visible and palpable things, the spirit in its high-flown arrogance would be sheer madness. The body is the tutor and the policeman of the spirit.

Hence the exemplary character of physical thinking among all other intellectual activities. Physics owes its unique strength to the fact that it has been the only science in which the truth is established through the accord of two independent instances, neither of which will let itself be bribed by the other: pure mathematical thinking *a priori* and pure observation of nature with the body's eye; analysis and experiment.

The founding fathers of the *nuova scienza* were well aware that it was made of the same stuff as technology —Bacon as well as Galileo, Gilbert and Descartes, Huygens, Hooke and Newton.

Since their time, in no more than three centuries, the development of both, science and technology, has been miraculous. But human life is not only a struggle with nature; it is also the struggle of man with his soul. What has Euramerica contributed to the techniques of the soul? Can it be that in this realm it is inferior to unfathomable Asia? Let us conclude our argument with opening a vista on future investigations which would have to confront Asiatic technologies with those of Western civilization.

4

History as a System

I

HUMAN life is a strange reality concerning which the first thing to be said is that it is the basic reality, in the sense that to it we must refer all others, since all others, effective or presumptive, must in one way or another appear within it.

The most trivial and at the same time the most important note in human life is that man has no choice but to be always doing something to keep himself in existence. Life is given to us; we do not give it to ourselves, rather we find ourselves in it, suddenly and without knowing how. But the life which is given us is not given us ready-made; we must make it for ourselves, each one his own. Life is a task. And the weightiest aspect of these tasks in which life consists is not the necessity of performing them but, in a sense, the opposite: I mean that we find ourselves always under compulsion to do something but never, strictly speaking, under compulsion to do something in particular, that there is not imposed on us this or that task as there is imposed on the star its course or on the stone its gravitation. Each individual before doing anything must decide for himself and at his own risk what he is going to do. But this decision is impossible unless one possesses certain convictions concerning the nature of things around one, the nature of other men, of oneself. Only in the light of such convictions can one prefer one act to another, can one, in short, live.

It follows that man must ever be grounded on some belief, and that the structure of his life will depend primordially on the beliefs on which he is grounded; and further that the most decisive changes in humanity are changes of belief, the intensifying or weakening of beliefs. The diagnosis of any human existence, whether of an individual, a people, or an age, must begin by establishing the repertory of its convictions. For always in living one sets out from certain convictions. They are the ground beneath our feet, and it is for this reason we say that man is grounded on them. It is man's beliefs that truly constitute his state. I have spoken of them as a repertory to indicate that the plurality of beliefs on which an individual, a people, or an age is grounded never possesses a completely logical articulation, that is to say, does not form a system of ideas such as, for example, a philosophy constitutes or aims at constituting. The beliefs that coexist in any human life, sustaining, impelling, and directing it, are on occasion incongruous, contradictory, at the least confused. Be it noted that all these qualifications attach to beliefs in so far as they partake of ideas. But it is erroneous to define belief as an idea. Once an idea has been thought it has exhausted its role and its consistency. The individual, moreover, may think whatever the whim suggests to him, and even many things against his whim. Thoughts arise in the mind spontaneously, without will or deliberation on our part and without producing any effect whatever on our behavior. A belief is not merely an idea that is thought, it is an idea in which one also believes. And believing is not an operation of the intellectual mechanism, but a function of the living being as such, the function of guiding his conduct, his performance of his task.

This observation once made, I can now withdraw my previous expression and say that beliefs, a mere incoherent repertory in so far as they are merely ideas, always constitute a system in so far as they are effective beliefs; in other words, that while lacking articulation from the logical or strictly intellectual point of view, they do nonetheless possess a vital articulation, they *function* as beliefs resting one on another, combining with one another to form a whole: in short, that they always present themselves as members of an organism, of a structure. This causes them among other things always to possess their own architecture and to function as a hierarchy. In every human life there are beliefs that are basic, fundamental, radical, and there are others derived from these, upheld by them, and secondary to them. If this observation is supremely trivial, the fault is not mine that with all its triviality it remains of the greatest importance. For should the beliefs by which one lives lack structure, since their number in each individual life is legion there must result a mere pullulation hostile to all idea of order and incomprehensible in consequence.

The fact that we should see them, on the contrary, as endowed with a structure and a hierarchy allows us to penetrate their hidden order and consequently to understand our own life and the life of others, that of today and that of other days.

Thus we may now say that the diagnosing of any human existence, whether of an individual, a people, or an age, must begin by an ordered inventory of its system of convictions, and to this end it must establish before all else which belief is fundamental, decisive, sustaining and breathing life into all the others.

Now in order to determine the state of one's beliefs at a given moment the only method we possess is that of comparing this moment with one or more other moments.

The more numerous the terms of comparison the more exact will be the result—another banal observation whose far-reaching consequences will emerge suddenly at the end of this meditation.

II

A comparison of the state of beliefs in which the European finds himself today with that obtaining a mere thirty years ago makes it clear that this has changed profoundly, because the fundamental conviction has changed.

The generation that flourished about the year 1900 was the last of a very long cycle, a cycle which began towards the end of the sixteenth century and was characterized by the fact that men lived on their faith in reason. In what does this faith consist?

If we open the *Discours de la Méthode,* the classical program of the new age, we find that it culminates in the following sentences:

Those long chains of simple and easy conclusions used by the geometricians for obtaining their most difficult proofs made me think that everything within the ken of man is interlaced in this same manner and that, if only we refrain from accepting as true what may be not true and from upsetting the order required for deducing one thing from the other, there can be nothing so remote that it will not finally be reached nor so hidden that it will not be discovered.[1]

[1] *Œuvres,* ed. Adam et Tannery, vol. 6, p. 19.

These words are the cockcrow of rationalism, the moving reveille that ushers in a whole new age, our so-called modern age, that modern age whose death agony, whose swan song, as it seems to many, we are today witnessing.

There is at least no denying that between the Cartesian attitude of mind and our own no slight difference exists. What joy, what a tone of vigorous challenge to the universe, what an early-morning presumptuousness these magnificent words of Descartes reveal! The reader has observed: apart from the divine mysteries which his courtesy bids him leave on one side, to this man there is no problem that cannot be solved. He assures us that in the universe there are no arcana, no unconquerable secrets before which humanity must halt in defenseless terror. The world that surrounds man all about, existence within which constitutes his life, is to become transparent, even to its farthest recesses, to the human mind. At last man is to know the truth about everything. It suffices that he should not lose heart at the complexity of the problems, and that he should allow no passion to cloud his mind. If with serene self-mastery he uses the apparatus of his intellect, if in particular he uses it in orderly fashion, he will find that his faculty of thought is *ratio*, reason, and that in reason he possesses the almost magic power of reducing everything to clarity, of turning what is most opaque to crystal, penetrating it by analysis until it is become self-evident. According to this, the world of reality and the world of thought are each a cosmos corresponding one to the other, each compact and continuous, wherein nothing is abrupt, isolated, or inaccessible, but rather such that from any point in it we may without intermission and without leaping pass to all other points and contemplate the whole. Man with his reason may thus plunge tranquilly into the abysmal depths of the universe, certain of extracting from the remotest problem, from the closest enigma, the essence of its truth, even as the Coromandel diver plunges into the deeps of ocean to reappear straightway bearing between his teeth the pearl of great price.

In the closing years of the sixteenth century and these early years of the seventeenth in which Descartes is meditating Western man believes, then, that the world possesses a rational structure, that is to say, that reality possesses an organization coincident with the organization of the human intellect, taking this, of course, in its purest form, that of mathematical reason. Here accordingly is a marvelous key giving man a power over things around him that is theoretically illimitable. Such a discovery was a pretty stroke of fortune. For suppose that Europe had not then come by this belief. In the fifteenth century it had lost its faith in God, in revelation, either because man had completely lost that faith or because it had ceased to be in him a living faith. Theologians make a very shrewd distinction, one capable of throwing light on not a few things of today, between a live and a sluggish faith. Generalizing this, I should formulate it thus: we believe in something with a live faith when that belief is sufficient for us to live by, and we believe in something with a dead, a sluggish faith when, without having abandoned it, being still grounded on it, it no longer acts efficaciously on our lives. It is become a drag, a dead weight; still part of us, yet useless as lumber in the attic of the soul. We no longer rest our existence on that something believed in; the stimuli, the pointers we live by no longer spring spontaneously from that faith. The proof is that we are constantly forgetting we still believe in it, whereas a living faith is the constant and most active presence of the entity we believe in. (Hence the perfectly natural phenomenon that the mystic calls "the presence of God." For a living love is likewise distinguished from a lifeless, dragging love in this, that the object loved is present to us without need of trance or fear of eclipse. We do not need to go in search of it with our attention; on the contrary, we have difficulty in removing it from before our inner eye. And this is not to say that we are always nor even frequently *thinking* about it, but simply that we constantly "count on it.")

An illustration of this difference in the present situation of the European I shall shortly adduce.[2]

Throughout the Middle Ages the European had lived on revelation. Lacking it, limited to his own naked strength, he would have felt incapable of dealing with the mysterious surroundings that made up his world, with the misfortunes and trials of existence. But he believed with a living faith that an all-powerful, all-knowing being would unfold to him gratuitously all that was essential to his life. We may follow the vicissitudes of this faith and witness, almost generation by generation, its progressive decay. It is a melancholy story. Gradually the living faith ceases to take nutriment, loses its color, becomes paralyzed, until, from whatever motives —these lie outside my present inquiry—towards the middle of the fifteenth century that living faith is clearly seen to have changed to a tired, ineffective faith, if indeed the individual soul has not uprooted it entirely. The man of that age begins to perceive that revelation does not suffice to illumine his relations to the world; once more he is conscious of being lost in the trackless forest of the universe, face to face with which he lacks alike a guide and a mediator. The fifteenth and the six-

[2] In his book *On Liberty*, chap. 2, John Stuart Mill makes very opportune use of this same distinction, expressed in the same terms of "living faith" and "dead, inert faith."

teenth centuries are, therefore, two centuries of tremendous restlessness, of fierce disquiet, two centuries, as we should say today, of crisis. From this crisis Western man is saved by a new faith, a new belief: faith in reason, in the *nuove scienze*. Man, having again fallen, is born again. The Renaissance is the parturient disquiet of a new confidence based on physico-mathematical science, the new mediator between man and the world.

III

Beliefs constitute the basic stratum, that which lies deepest, in the architecture of our life. By them we live, and by the same token we rarely think of them. Whatever is still to us more or less in debate, that we think of. Hence we say that we *hold* such and such ideas, whereas rather than holding our beliefs we are them.

One may symbolize the individual life as a bank of issue. The bank lives on the credit of a gold reserve which is rarely seen, which lies at the bottom of metal coffers hidden in the vaults of the building. The most elementary caution will suggest that from time to time the effective condition of these guaranties—of these *credences*, one might say, that are the basis of *credit*—be passed in review.

Today it is become urgent that we should do the same with the faith in reason by which the European, obedient

to tradition—a tradition of close on three centuries—
has been living. It may be said that until twenty years
ago the state of this belief had not suffered modification
in its general outline, but that in the last few years it has
changed most profoundly. So much is demonstrated by
innumerable facts, facts that are only too well known
and that it would be depressing to enunciate once more.

It will be superfluous to point out that in speaking of
the traditional faith in reason and of its present-day
modification I am not referring to what happens in this
or that individual as such. Apart from what individuals
as individuals, that is to say, each for himself and on
his own account, may believe, there exists always a collective state of belief. This social faith may or may not
coincide with that felt by such and such an individual.
The decisive factor in the matter is that whatever may
be the private belief of each one of us we are confronted
with a state of faith collectively constituted and established, a faith, in short, that is socially operative.

The faith in science to which I refer was not merely and
firstly an individual opinion. It was, on the contrary, a
collective opinion, and when something is a collective or
social opinion it is a reality independent of individuals,
outside them as the stones on the ground, a reality
with which individuals must reckon willy-nilly. Our personal opinion may run counter to social opinion, but this

will not invalidate one iota the reality of the latter. What constitutes and gives a specific character to collective opinion is the fact that its existence does not depend on its acceptance or rejection by any given individual. From the viewpoint of each individual life public belief has, as it were, the appearance of a physical object. The tangible reality, so to speak, of collective belief does not consist in its acceptance by you or by me; instead it is it which, whether we acquiesce or not, imposes on us its reality and forces us to reckon with it. To this characteristic of social faith I apply the term "operative." A law is said to be operative when, far from its effectiveness hinging on my recognition of it, it acts and functions independently of my adhesion. And in like manner collective belief has no need of my belief in it as a particular individual in order to exist and weigh upon me and even, perchance, crush me. If now it be agreed, for our better understanding, to apply the term "social dogma" to the content of a collective belief, we are in a position to continue our meditation.

When, equipped with these instrumental concepts, we compare the situation in which the European found himself about the year 1910 with that of today, the perception of the change, the mutation, that has occurred ought to cause in us a salutary terror. A mere twenty years, that is to say only a portion of a man's life, in itself so short, have sufficed to invert the order of things to the point that, whereas then one might in any part of Europe have invoked faith in science and the rights of science as the maximum human value, and this urge functioned automatically, the social body accepting in all docility its imperative and reacting thereto with efficacy, energy, and promptitude, today there are already nations where such an invocation would provoke only smiles—nations that some years ago were considered precisely as being in the van of science—and I do not believe there is any, at the time of writing, in which it would call forth even a throb from the social body.

IV

Science is in danger. In saying this I do not think I exaggerate. For this is not to say that Europe collectively has made a radical end of its belief in science, but only that its faith, once living, is in our day become sluggish. This is sufficient to cause science to be in danger and to make it impossible for the scientist to go on living as he has lived till now, sleepwalking at his work, believing that the society around him still supports, sustains, and venerates him. What has happened to bring about such a situation? Science today knows with incredible precision much of what is happening on remote stars and galaxies. Science is rightly proud of the fact, and because of it, although with less right, it spreads its peacock feathers at academic gatherings. But meanwhile it has come about that this same science, once a living social faith, is now almost looked down upon by society in general. And although this has not happened on Sirius but only on our own planet, it is not, I conceive, bereft of importance. Science cannot be merely science about Sirius; it claims also to be science about man. What then has science, reason, got to say today, with reasonable precision, concerning this so urgent fact that so intimately concerns it? Just nothing. Science has no clear knowledge on the matter. One perceives the enormity of the position, the shame of it. The upshot is that, where great human changes are concerned, science, strictly so called, has got nothing exact to say. The thing is so enormous that it straightway reveals to us the reason. For it causes us to note that the science, the reason, in which modern man placed his social faith is, speaking strictly, merely physico-mathematical science together with biological science, the latter based directly on the former and benefiting, in its weakness, from the other's prestige —in short, summing both up together, what is called natural science or reason.

The present position of physical science or reason is in consequence somewhat paradoxical. If there is anything in the repertory of human activities and pursuits that has not proved a failure, it is precisely this science, when one considers it circumscribed within its genuine territory, nature. Within this order and ambit, far from having failed, it has transcended all our hopes. For the first time in history the powers of realization, of achievement, have outstripped those of mere fantasy. Science has achieved things that irresponsible imaginings had never so much as dreamed of. This is so unquestionable that one has difficulty in understanding straightway why man is not today on his knees before science as before some magic power. The fact remains that he is not on his knees; on the contrary, he is beginning to turn his back. He does not deny, he is not unaware of, its marvelous power, its triumph over nature, but he realizes at the same time that nature is only one dimension of human life and that a resounding success with regard to nature does not preclude failure with regard to the totality of our existence. Life at any instant is an inexorable balance, in which "physical reason" (*la razón física*) for all its partial splendor does not rule out the possibility of a heavy deficit. Even more, the lack of equilibrium between the perfection of its partial efficiency and its failure from the comprehensive point of view, which is final, is such in my opinion that it has contributed to the aggravation of our universal disquiet.

Man thus finds himself, when confronted with physical reason, in a state of mind comparable to that of Christina of Sweden, as described by Leibnitz, when, after her abdication, she caused a coin to be struck bearing the effigy of a crown and had these words inscribed in the exergue: *Non mi bisogna e non mi basta.*

In the upshot the paradox resolves itself into a supremely simple observation. What has not collapsed in physics is physics. What has collapsed in it is the rhetoric, the trimmings of childish presumption, of irrational and arbitrary additions it gave rise to, what, many years ago, I styled "the terrorism of the laboratory." This is why ever since I began to write I have combated what I called scientific *Utopianism.* Open, for example, *El tema de nuestro tiempo* at the chapter entitled "The historic sense of Einstein's theory," written about 1921. There the following passage will be found:

It is incomprehensible that science, whose only pleasure lies in attaining to a true image of things, should nourish itself on illusions. I recall a detail whose influence on my thought was decisive. Many years ago I was reading a lecture of the physiologist Loeb on tropism. The tropism is a concept which has been invoked to describe and throw light on the law governing the elemental movements of the infusoria. The concept serves, indifferently well and with corrections and additions, to help us understand some of these phenomena. But at the close of this lecture Loeb adds: "The day will come when what we now call moral acts in man will be explained simply as tropisms." Such temerity perturbed me exceedingly, for it opened my eyes to many other judgments of modern science that are guilty, if less ostentatiously, of the same error. So then, I thought, a concept like the tropism, which is scarce capable of plumbing the secret of phenomena so simple as the antics of the infusoria, may at some vague future date suffice to explain phenomena as mysterious and complex as man's ethical acts! What sense is there here? Science has to solve its problems in the present, not transport us to the Greek kalends. If its present methods are insufficient to master now the enigmas of the universe, discretion would suggest that they be replaced by other and more effective ones. But the science *à la mode* is full of problems which are left intact because they are incompatible with its methods. As if it was the former that were under obligation to subordinate themselves to the latter, and not the other way round! Science is full of achronisms, of Greek kalends.

When we emerge from a science so devoutly simple, bowing in idolatrous worship before pre-established methods, and approach the thought of Einstein there comes upon us as it were a fresh morning breeze. Einstein's attitude is radically different from that of tradition. With the dash of a young athlete we see him make straight for his problems and take them by the horns, using the method that lies nearest to his hand. Out of the apparent defects and limitations of science he draws virtue and tactical efficiency.

From this idea of the Greek kalends all my philosophic thought has emanated. There in germ is my whole conception of life as the basic reality and of knowledge as an internal—and not an independent or Utopian— function of life. Just as Einstein was then telling us that in physics it is necessary to elaborate concepts such as will make absolute motion impossible (absolute motion is immeasurable and before what cannot be measured physics is impotent), I considered it essential to elaborate a philosophy that should take its point of departure, its formal principle, from the exclusion of the Greek kalends. Because life is the opposite of these kalends. Life is haste and has urgent need to know what it is up against, and it is out of this urgency that truth must derive its method. The idea of progress, placing truth in a vague tomorrow, has proved a dulling opiate to humanity. Truth is what is true now and not what remains to be discovered in an undetermined future. Mr. Loeb—and his whole generation is with him—gives up his claim to a present truth of morality on the strength of the future attaining to a physics of morality: a curious way of existing at the expense of posterity while leaving one's own life shorn of foundations, of roots, of any profound implications in the scheme of things. The viciousness of this attitude is so radical that it appears already in the "provisional morality" of Descartes. And so it happens that the first blow directed against the superficial framework of our civilization, our economics, our morals, our politics, finds man possessed of no truths of his own, of no clear, firm position on anything of importance.

The only thing he believed in was physical science, and when this received the urgent call to propound its truth on the most human problems, it did not know what to say. And suddenly Western man has received the impression of losing his footing, of finding himself without support, and has known a panic terror and believed himself to be sinking, making shipwreck in the void.

And yet, a measure of serenity is all that is needed for our feet once more to experience the delicious sensation of touching hard, solid mother earth, an element capable of sustaining man. As always, it is essential— and sufficient—instead of giving way to panic and losing one's head, to convert into a source of support the very factor that had engendered the impression of an abyss. Physical science can throw no clear light on the human element. Very well. This means simply that we must shake ourselves free, radically free, from the physical, the natural, approach to the human element. Let us instead accept this in all its spontaneity, just as we see it and come upon it. In other words, the collapse of physical reason leaves the way clear for vital, historical reason.[3]

V

Nature is a thing, a great thing, that is composed of many lesser things. Now, whatever be the differences between things, they all have one basic feature in common, which consists simply in the fact that things *are,* they

[3] The form I first gave to this thought, in my youth, may be found in *El tema de nuestro tiempo,* 1923 (English translation by James Cleugh. 1932).

have their being. And this signifies not only that they exist, that there they are, in front of us, but also that they possess a given, fixed structure or consistency. Given a stone, there exists forthwith, for all to see, what a stone is. Its every change and mutation, world without end, will be in specific combinations of its fundamental consistency. The stone can never be something new and different. This consistency, given and fixed once and for all, is what we customarily understand when we speak of the being of a thing. An alternative expression is the word "nature." And the task of natural science is to penetrate beneath changing appearances to that permanent nature or texture.

When naturalist reason studies man it seeks, in consistence with itself, to reveal his nature. It observes that man has a body, which is a thing, and hastens to submit it to physics; and since this body is also an organism, it hands it over to biology. It observes further that in man as in animals there functions a certain mechanism incorporeally, confusedly attached to the body, the psychic mechanism, which is also a thing, and entrusts its study to psychology, a natural science. But the fact is that this has been going on for three hundred years and that all the naturalist studies on man's body and soul put together have not been of the slightest use in throwing light on any of our most strictly human feelings, on what each individual calls his own life, that life which, intermingling with others, forms societies, that in their turn, persisting, make up human destiny. The prodigious achievement of natural science in the direction of the knowledge of things contrasts brutally with the collapse of this same natural science when faced with the strictly human element. The human element escapes physico-mathematical reason as water runs from a sieve.

And here we have the explanation why our faith in reason has entered upon a phase of lamentable decadence. Man cannot wait any longer. He demands that science illumine for him the problems of humanity. At bottom he is somewhat tired by now of stars and nervous reactions and atoms. The earliest generations of rationalists believed that with their physical science they could throw light on human destiny. Descartes himself wrote a treatise *De homine*. Today we know that all the marvels of the natural sciences, inexhaustible though they be in principle, must always come to a full stop before the strange reality of human life. Why? If all things have given up a large part of their secret to physical science, why does this alone hold out so stoutly? The explanation must go deep, down to the roots. Perchance it is no less than this: that man is not a thing, that it is false to talk of human nature, that man has no nature. I conceive that a physicist, on hearing this, may well feel his hair stand on end, since it signifies, in other words, an assertion that physics is radically incompetent to speak of man. But it is useless to shelter behind illusions: whether our consciousness of this be clear or not so clear, whether we suspect or not the existence of another mode of knowledge, another reason capable of speaking of man, the conviction of this incompetence is today a fact of the first magnitude on the European horizon. Physicists in the presence of it may feel irritated or pained—although both attitudes may here seem somewhat puerile—but this conviction is the historical precipitate of three centuries of failure.

Human life, it would appear then, is not a thing, has not a nature, and in consequence we must make up our minds to think of it in terms of categories and concepts that will be *radically* different from such as shed light on the phenomena of matter. The enterprise is no easy one, since for the last three centuries "physicism" has accustomed us to leaving behind us, as an entity having neither importance nor reality, precisely this strange reality of human life. And so, while the naturalists devoted themselves with pious absorption to their professional tasks, the whim has taken this strange reality to veer to another point of the compass, and on enthusiasm for science there have followed lukewarmness and aversion. Tomorrow, who knows, it may be frank hostility.

VI

It will be said that the more patent became the resistance of the human phenomenon to physical science, the more prominent became another form of science opposed to this: against the natural sciences, in effect, there arose and developed the so-called sciences of the spirit, the moral or cultural sciences. To this I reply, to begin with, that these sciences of the spirit, *Geisteswissenschaften*, have not so far been successful in moving the European to belief in the way that the natural sciences were.

And this is easily understood. The representatives of the spiritual sciences were combating the avowed intent of the others to investigate the human element by means of naturalistic ideas; but it happens that the spiritual sciences have in fact represented so far no more than a disguised attempt to do the same. Let me explain.

Geist? Wer ist der Bursche? asked Schopenhauer, with an ill-humored insolence that was not lacking in common sense. This great Utopian concept of the spirit sought to oppose itself to nature. One felt intuitively that nature was not the only reality and, above all, that it was not the primary or fundamental one. The more one got to grips with it, the more it appeared to depend on the human element. German idealism, like the positivism of Comte, signifies the attempt to place man before nature. It was the former that gave man, in so far as he is not nature, the name *Geist*, spirit.

But it happened that in the effort to comprehend the human element as a spiritual reality things did not go any better: human phenomena showed the same resistance, the same stubborn reluctance to let themselves be hemmed in by concepts. Further, it was a privilege reserved to the thought of that age to indulge in the most scandalous and irresponsible Utopias. One readily appreciates Schopenhauer's ill-humor and insolence. Hegel's *Philosophy of History* and Comte's "law of the three estates" are, beyond a doubt, two works of genius. In affixing to them this qualification of genius, however, all we are clearly doing is to applaud a man's magnificent dexterity as such, to applaud him for his agility, for what he has of the juggler or the athlete. If we study these works, chiefly Hegel's, from the decisive point of view, that of intellectual responsibility, and consider them as symptomatic of a moral climate, we soon perceive that they would have been impossible, *ceteris paribus*, in any normal epoch of thought, in any age of restraint, proportion, and sensitive respect for the function of the intellect.

I am bold to say this solely as an extrinsic indication of the fact that the interpretation of man as a spiritual reality could not but be violent, arbitrary, and a failure. Because in this context it is not permissible to continue using the word "spirit" vaguely; it must needs be referred to the cycle of exact meanings it has borne in the philosophy of the past two centuries.

If now we ask why the concept of spirit has shown itself insufficient to explain the human element we are led to the following fundamental consideration.

When the knights-errant of the spirit sallied forth to wage war on naturalism, determined to give a scrupulous representation of human phenomena in their genuine essence and putting far from them the concepts and categories that nature imposes on our thinking, they did not take heed that, as they set out, they had already left the enemy behind. In nature they saw only certain peculiar attributes, spatiality, force, their sensorial manifestation, and the like, and they believed it sufficient to replace these by other antagonistic attributes, *cogitatio*, consciousness, apperception, and the like, in order to place themselves outside nature. In short, they were guilty of the same mistake Descartes made when he held it enough, in order to define the self, to oppose it as a *res cogitans* to the *res extensa*. But can the fundamental difference between that strange reality, man, the *ego*, and that other reality, things, consist in the fact that the *ego* thinks while things have extent? What difficulty

would there be in the *res* that thinks having extent and
the *res* that has extent thinking? Descartes is wont to
add, astutely, that the *res* that thinks has no extent and
the *res* that has extent does not think. But this denial,
coming as an afterthought, is wholly arbitrary, and Spi-
noza, who was not easily imposed upon, calmly draws
the inference that one and the same *res—Natura sive
Deus*—thinks and has extent. To compose the issue it
would be necessary to do what Descartes did not do, to
wit, to ask oneself what is this *res* business, what is its
structure, before proceeding to classify it as thinking or
as having extent. For if the attributes of *cogitatio* and
extensio are in such wise antagonistic that they cannot
coexist in the same *res,* the suspicion arises that each of
them must react on the very structure of the *res* as *res.*
Or, which comes to the same thing, that the term *res* is
equivocal in both expressions.

Now, the concept *res* had already been established by
traditional ontology. The error made by Descartes and by
the knights-errant of the spirit lay in not carrying down
to bedrock their reform of philosophy, in applying un-
thinkingly to the new reality they aspired to establish—
pensée, Geist—the old doctrine of being. Can an entity
that consists in thinking have *being* in the same sense as
one that consists in having extent has *being?* Apart from
the difference implied in the fact that one thinks while

the other has extent, are they not differentiated also in their very being, as entities *sensu stricto?*

In traditional ontology the term *res* is always linked with the term *natura,* whether as a synonym or in the sense that *natura* is the real *res,* the beginning of *res.* The concept of nature we know to be of pure Greek descent: it is first stabilized in Aristotle, then, modified by the Stoics, it comes into the Renaissance, and through that mighty portal inundates the modern age. In Robert Boyle it finds the expression that still holds: *"natura* is the rule or system of rules according to which phenomena behave—in short, their law." [4]

To go back over the history of the concept of nature is not possible here, and any summary of it must be futile. For the sake of brevity I shall content myself with a single allusion: is it not surprising that the term "nature" should have come, with unbroken continuity, from meaning what it meant to Aristotle to mean the law of phenomena? Is not the distance between the two meanings enormous? That distance, be it noted, implies nothing less than the whole change in our way of thinking of the universe from ancient to modern man. What then, down this long evolution, has remained constant in the concept of nature?

<hr />

[4] Cassirer, *Das Erkenntnisproblem in der Philosophie und Wissenschaft der neueren Zeit,* vol. 2, p. 433.

There are few themes in which one may see so clearly as here the extent to which European man is heir to the Greek. Inheritance, however, is not only treasure; it is, at the same time, a charge and a bond. Concealed in the concept of nature we have received the bonds that make us the slaves of Hellenic destiny.

Greek thought is formulated in Parmenides. Parmenides represents beyond question the pure essence of Hellenism, for it is a fact that Eleaticism has always held sway in Hellenic minds. What was not Eleaticism, simple or compound, was merely opposition. This Greek destiny continues to weigh on us, and in spite of some notable rebellions we are still prisoners within the magic circle described by Eleatic ontology.

Ever since Parmenides, the orthodox thinker in search of an object's being holds that he is searching for a fixed, static consistency,[5] hence something that the entity *already* is, which already composes or constitutes it. The prototype of this mode of being, possessed of the characteristics of fixity, stability, and actuality (a being *already* what it is), was the being of mathematical concepts and objects, an invariable being, a being-always-the-same. Since observation showed that the things in the world around were changeable, were "movement," he

---

[5] Alongside the term *existence* I use that of *consistency*. The entity that *exists* has a consistency, that is to say, it *consists of* something or other.

begins by denying their reality. Aristotle, more prudent, renounces such absolutism and adopts a solution of the *juste milieu*. In the changeable object he seeks that which in the midst of change does not vary, that which in its movement remains motionless. This accordingly is what he called the "nature" of things, that which in the real object *appears* to shrink from having a being similar to the being of mathematical concepts and objects. The φύσις was the invariable principle of variations. In this way it became possible to retain the fundamental Eleaticism of being and yet to conceive as realities those objects which in the eyes of absolute Eleaticism lacked authentic reality, οὐσία. The idea of time, interposing itself between the invariable οὐσία and the diverse states of the object, served as a bridge between the latent unity of being and its apparent multiplicity. The *res* was thus conceived of as something possessing at heart—in its ἀρχή—the same ontological condition as the concept and the triangle: identity, radical invariability, stability—the profound tranquillity that the term *being* signified to the Greek.

The process that causes the *natura* of Aristotelianism to evolve into Boyle's stable rule or law of unstable phenomena, far from being a degeneration, is a purification of the original concept and as it were a sincere confession of it. Thus in Comte and Stuart Mill everything hangs as from a nail on "the invariability of the laws of nature."

The nature of positivism is already pure and declared "invariability," a being fixed, static . . . Eleatic.[6]

Now, in laying down as a condition of reality, before admitting it as such, that it should consist in an element of identity, Parmenides and the orthodox Greeks in general revealed their colossal arbitrariness. Into the origin of what I call sublime "arbitrariness" I do not propose here to inquire, although the theme is one of infinite attractiveness. The word is an express concept, and the concept is a reality that is peculiar among realities in consisting of identity, one might say in being made of identity. When we speak of reality—*onto-logy*—we are under obligation to be faithful at once to the conditions of the reality of which we are thinking and to the conditions of the thought with which we "manipulate" the reality.

One can readily understand that philosophy, in its first phase, should have lacked the agility necessary to distinguish, in thinking of reality, between that element in the resulting thought that belonged to the intellect and that which belonged properly to the object. Until Kant, strictly speaking, no one had even begun to see clearly that thought is not a copy and mirror of reality but a transitive operation performed on it, a surgical intervention.

---

[6] I do not enter here into the question whether this is compatible with the relativism of Comte. This is a theme which I hope to develop in a forthcoming study on *The Unknown Comte*.

Hence philosophy since Kant has embarked on what Plato would call its δεύτερος πλοῦς, its second voyage, its second apprenticeship. This rests on the observation that if there be possible a knowledge of authentic reality, αὐτὸ τὸ ὄν (and only philosophic knowledge claims to be such), it must consist in a duplicate thinking, a going and coming —that is to say, in a thinking that, having once thought something concerning reality, turns back on the thought and strips it of what is mere intellectual form, leaving only the intuition of reality in all its nakedness. This is fearsome, and paradoxical, but there is no other way out. In the formidable crusade for the liberation of man that constitutes the mission of the intellect there has come a moment when man needs to deliver himself from his most intimate slavery, to wit, from himself. It follows from this that, precisely because Kant has taught us that thought has its own forms and projects these on to the real, the end of the process initiated by him consists in uprooting from reality all those forms that are at once inevitable and foreign to it, and in learning to think with a mind ever on the alert, in an unceasing *modus ponendo tollens*. In short, we must learn to disintellectualize the real if we are to be faithful to it.

Eleaticism was the radical intellectualization of being. It is this that constitutes the magic circle already referred to, that we so urgently need to rise above. In naturalism what prevents our conceiving of human phenomena, what veils them to our minds, is not the secondary attributes of things, *res*, but the very idea of *res* founded on identical being and, since identical, fixed, static, predetermined. Wherever this subtle attribute persists, there naturalism, invariable being, is still to be found. Naturalism is, at bottom, intellectualism, i. e., the projection on to the real of the mode of being peculiar to concepts. Let us renounce valiantly, joyously, this convenient presumption that the real is logical and recognize that thought alone is logical.[7] Even the mathematical object presents chasms of illogicality as tremendous as the "labyrinth of the difficulties of continuity" and all the problems that inspired Brouwer's attempt to overthrow the *principium tertii exclusi*. Today physics, too, has sprung a dramatic surprise on us with its states of indeterminateness of the atomic elements.

This article, I need not point out, is not a treatise, quite the contrary; it is a series of theses that are submitted without defense to the meditative fair play of the reader. I believe nonetheless that some meaning will now attach to my previous enigmatic assertion according to which the concept of spirit is a disguised naturalism and in con-

[7] *Vide* " 'La Filosofía de la Historia' de Hegel y la historiología," *Revista de Occidente*, February, 1928.

sequence inoperative when faced with naturalistic conceptions, its presumed enemies.

Spirit, if it is anything in this world, is identity, and hence *res*, a thing—though as subtle and ethereal as you please. Spirit possesses a static consistency: it is already, to begin with, what it is going to be. The revolt of the human element against any conception of it as static was so obvious that soon, with Leibnitz, there came the attempt to rise above the static by making spirit consist in dynamic activity.[8] A vain attempt, for that activity, like all activity, is always one and the same, fixed, prescribed, ontologically motionless! Hegel's movement of the spirit is a pure fiction, since it is a movement within the spirit, whose consistency lies in its fixed, static, pre-established truth. Now the entity whose being consists in identical being evidently possesses already, to begin with, all it needs in order to be. For this reason identical being is substantive being, substance, a being that suffices to itself, sufficient being. This is the *thing*. Spirit is no other than a thing. It appears indeed that other things are things in virtue of their materiality, their spatiality, their force. But all this would serve them in no stead if they were not

---

[8] Only Fichte constitutes a case apart. One is aware that he touches the true being of life, but his intellectualism does not allow him to see what it is he is touching, and he is compelled forcibly to think Eleatically. Whence the pathetic resemblance to a blind traveler we see in Fichte as he journeys across the mountain ranges of metaphysics.

also and previously identical, *that is to say, concepts*. The *proto*-thing, the *Urding*, is the intellect. It identi-fies, thing-ifies—*ver-dinglicht*—all the rest.

The knights-errant of the spirit have no right to the revulsion, that amusing Plotinian revulsion, they feel where nature is concerned. Because the profound error of naturalism is the reverse of what is supposed: it does not consist in our treating ideas as though they were cor- poreal realities, but on the contrary in our treating real- ities—corporeal or no—as if they were ideas, concepts, in short, identities.

When Heine, assuredly after reading Hegel, asked his coachman, "What are ideas?" the answer he got was: "Ideas? . . . Ideas are the things they put into your head." But the fact is that we can say, more formally, that things are the ideas that come out of our heads and are taken by us as realities.

The need to rise above, to transcend the idea of nature comes precisely from this, that this idea can have no va- lidity as an authentic reality: it is something relative to the human intellect, which in its turn has no detached, in- dependent reality—herein lies the error of all idealism or "spiritualism"—but is only real when functioning in a human life, by whose constitutive urgencies it is moved. Nature is a transitory interpretation that man has given to what he finds around him in life. To this then, as to a

radical reality, including and preforming all others, we
are referred.

Faced with this, what we are indeed now conscious of is
a liberation from naturalism, because we have learnt to
immunize ourselves from intellectualism and its Greek
kalends. Here is the "fact" previous to all facts, that
which holds all others in solution and from which all
flow: human life as it is lived by each one of us. *Hic
Rhodus, hic salta.* Our need is to think on it with urgency,
just as we behold it in all its primary nakedness, by the
aid of concepts bent only on describing it and which admit no imperative whatever from traditional ontology.

That undertaking, needless to say, is not one that can
be pursued within the bounds of the present article. My
purpose here is limited to the suggestion of so much as is
indispensable if my title—"History as a System"—is to
have an exact meaning.

VII

Physico-mathematical reason, whether in its crude
form of naturalism or in its beatific form of spiritualism,
was in no state to confront human problems. By its very
constitution it could do no other than search for man's nature. And, naturally, it did not find it. For man has no
nature. Man is not his body, which is a thing, nor his soul,
psyche, conscience, or spirit, which is also a thing. Man

is no thing, but a drama—his life, a pure and universal happening which happens to each one of us and in which each one in his turn is nothing but happening. All things, be they what they may, are now mere interpretations which he exercises himself in giving to whatever he comes upon. Things he does not come upon: he poses or supposes them. What he comes upon are pure difficulties and pure facilities for existing. Existence itself is not presented to him ready-made, as it is to the stone; rather, shall we say, looping the loop begun in the opening words of this article, on coming up against the fact of his existence, on existence happening to him, all he comes up against, all that happens to him is the realization that he has no choice but to do something in order not to cease existing. This shows that the mode of being of life, even as simple existing, is not a *being already*, since the only thing that is given us and that *is* when there is human life is the having to make it, each one for himself.[9] Life is a gerundive, not a participle: a *faciendum*, not a *factum*. Life is a task. Life, in fact, sets us plenty of tasks. When

[9] Bergson, the least Eleatic of thinkers, whom we must allow today to have been right on so many points, constantly uses the expression *l'être en se faisant*. But a comparison of his sense with that which I here give to the same words shows a radical difference. In Bergson the term *se faisant* is merely a synonym of *devenir*. In my text *making oneself* is not merely *becoming* but in addition the way in which human reality *becomes*, which is the effective and literal *making oneself*, a *fabricating oneself*, we might say.

the doctor, surprised at Fontenelle's having reached the age of a hundred in full health, asked him what he felt, the centenarian replied: *Rien, rien du tout . . . seulement une certaine difficulté d'être.* We ought to generalize and say that life always, and not only at a hundred, consists in *difficulté d'être.* Its mode of being is formally a being difficult, a being which consists in problematic toil. Compared with the sufficient being of the substance or thing, life is an indigent being, an entity which possesses, properly speaking, only needs, *Bedürfnisse.* The star, on the other hand, continues ever on the line of its orbit, asleep like a child in the cradle.

At every moment of my life there open before me divers possibilities: I can do this or that. If I do this, I shall be A the moment after; if I do that, I shall be B. At the present moment the reader may stop reading me or may go on. And, however slight the importance of this article, according as he does the one or the other the reader will be A or will be B, will have made of himself an A or a B. Man is the entity that makes itself, an entity which traditional ontology only stumbled upon precisely as its course was drawing to a close, and which it in consequence gave up the attempt to understand: the *causa sui.* With this difference, that the *causa sui* had only to "exert itself" in being the *cause* of itself and not in determining what *self* it was going to cause. It had, to begin with, a *self* previously determined and invariable, consistent, for example, to infinity.

But man must not only make himself: the weightiest thing he has to do is to determine *what* he is going to be. He is *causa sui* to the second power. By a coincidence that is not casual, the doctrine of the living being, when it seeks in tradition for concepts that are still more or less valid, finds only those which the doctrine of the divine being tried to formulate. If the reader has resolved now to go on reading into the next moment, it will be, in the last instance, because doing this is what is most in accordance with the general program he has mapped out for his life, and hence with the man of determination he has resolved to be. This vital program is the *ego* of each individual, his choice out of divers possibilities of being which at every instant open before him.[10]

Concerning these possibilities of being the following remarks fall to be made:

1. That they likewise are not presented to me. I must find them for myself, either on my own or through the medium of those of my fellows with whom my life brings me in contact. I invent projects of being and of doing in the light of circumstance. This alone I come upon, this

[10] *Vide* my *Goethe desde dentro*, 1932.

alone is given me: circumstance.[11] It is too often forgotten that man is impossible without imagination, without the capacity to invent for himself a conception of life, to "ideate" the character he is going to be. Whether he be original or a plagiarist, man is the novelist of himself.[12]

2. That among these possibilities I must choose. Hence, I am free. But, be it well understood, I am free *by compulsion*, whether I wish to be or not. Freedom is not an activity pursued by an entity that, apart from and previous to such pursuit, is already possessed of a fixed being. To be free means to be lacking in constitutive identity, not to have subscribed to a determined being, to be able to be other than what one was, to be unable to install oneself once and for all in any given being. The only attribute of the fixed, stable being in the free being is this constitutive instability.

In order to speak, then, of man's being we must first elaborate a non-Eleatic concept of being, as others have elaborated a non-Euclidean geometry. The time has come for the seed sown by Heraclitus to bring forth its mighty harvest.

Man is an infinitely plastic entity of which one may

[11] Vide *Meditaciones del Quijote*, 1914. In this early book of mine it is already suggested that *I* am no more than one ingredient in that radical reality "my life," whose other ingredient is circumstance.
[12] Be it recalled that the Stoics spoke of an "imagining of oneself," φαντασία ἑαυτοῦ.

make what one will, precisely because of itself it is nothing save only the mere potentiality to be "as you like." Let the reader pass in review for a moment all the things that man has been—that is to say, that he has made of himself—and has then ceased to be—that is to say, has cast off from himself—from the paleolithic "savage" to the young *surréaliste* of Paris. I do not say that at any moment he may make of himself anything whatever. At each moment there open before him limited possibilities —what these limits are we shall see straightway. But if instead of one moment we take all moments, it is impossible to see what frontiers can be set to human plasticity. From the paleolithic female there have issued Madame Pompadour and Lucile de Chateaubriand, from the indigene of Brazil, unable to count above five, have come Newton and Henri Poincaré. Lessening the distance in time, be it remembered that in 1873 the liberal Stuart Mill, in 1903 the most liberal Herbert Spencer, were still alive, and that already in 1921 Stalin and Mussolini were in power.

Meanwhile man's body and psyche, his *nature*, have experienced no change of importance to which these effective mutations may be clearly ascribed. What has taken place, on the contrary, is the "substantial" change in the reality "human life" implied by man's passing from the belief that he must exist in a world composed only of arbitrary wills to the belief that he must exist in a world where there are "nature," invariable consistencies, identity, etc. Human life is thus not an entity that changes accidentally, rather the reverse: in it the "substance" is precisely change, which means that it cannot be thought of Eleatically as substance. Life being a "drama" that happens, and the "subject" to whom it happens being, not a thing apart from and previous to his drama, but a function of it, it follows that the "substance" of the drama would be its argument. And if this varies, it means that the variation is "substantial."

Since the being of whatever is alive is a being always distinct from itself—in the terms of the schools, a being that is metaphysically and not only physically mobile— it must be thought of in concepts that annul their own inevitable identity. This is not so terrifying as it may appear at first sight, though it is a question that I cannot even touch the fringe of here. I would only recall to the reader, that I may not leave his mind adrift on an uncharted sea, that thought has a much greater capacity for avoiding itself than is commonly supposed. Thought is constitutively generous, it is the great altruist. It is capable of thinking what lies at the opposite extreme to thought. One example will suffice. There are concepts called by some "occasional"; e. g., the concept "here," the concept "I," the concept "this." Such concepts or significations have a formal identity that serves precisely to guarantee the constitutive nonidentity of the matter signified or thought of through them. All concepts that seek to think of the authentic reality, life, must be "occasional" in this sense. There is nothing strange in this, since life is pure occasion. It is for this reason Cardinal Nicholas of Cusa calls man a *Deus occasionatus*, for, according to him, man once he is free is a creator like God inasmuch as he is a being creating its own entity. Unlike God, however, his creation is not absolute but is limited by the occasion. Whence, literally, what I am bold to affirm: that man makes himself in the light of circumstance, that he is a God as occasion offers, a "secondhand God" (*un Dios de ocasión*).

Every concept, in Husserl's phrase, is a universal meaning (*allgemeine Bedeutung*). But whereas in other concepts the universality consists in the fact that when applying them to one singular case we must always think the *same* as when applying them to another singular case, in the occasional concept it functions precisely by inviting us never to think the *same* when we apply it. The supreme example is this very concept "life" in the sense of human life. Its signification *qua* signification is, of course, identical, but what it signifies is something not merely singular, but unique. Life is the life of each one of us.

And here, for the sake of brevity, I may be allowed to

interrupt these considerations and to refrain from dealing with the most obvious difficulties they give rise to.[13]

VIII

Yesterday I made the acquaintance of Hermione. She
is a fascinating woman. Towards me she was deferential,
insinuating. I think of making love to her, and of attempting to win her love in return. But can my authentic being,
what I call *I,* consist in "being Hermione's lover"?
Scarcely have I conjured up my love for Hermione in
the mind's eye with a measure of precision when I emphatically turn down such a project of being. Why? I
can find no objection to raise against Hermione, only the
fact is . . . that I am fifty, and at fifty, although the
body may have retained all the elasticity of thirty and the
psychic impulses have lost none of their vigor, I cannot
now "be Hermione's lover." But why? The point is this,
that being a man of years I have already had time to be
the lover of Cidalisa and the lover of Arsinoe and the
lover of Glykeia, and I know now what "being a lover" is.

13 For example, whether two lives whose attributes were the same and,
in consequence, indistinguishable, would not be the *same* life. The idea
of life obliges us, in fact, to invert the Leibnitzian principle and to speak
of "the discernibility of identities." Or again, how, if life is unique, it is
at the same time multiple, since we can speak of the lives of others, etc.,
etc. All these difficulties are engendered in the old intellectualist habits.
The most interesting and fruitful of them consists in asking how it is that
we "define" life by means of general characteristics, saying that in all
its possible cases it is this and this and this.

I know its excellences, I know also its limitations. In short, I have experienced to the full that form of life that is called "loving a woman," and, frankly, I have had enough. And so it happens that the "cause" of my not being a lover tomorrow is precisely the fact that I have been one. If I had not been a lover, if I had not already experienced love to the full, I should be Hermione's lover.

Here, then, is a new dimension in this strange reality of life. Before us lie the diverse possibilities of being, but behind us lies what we have been. And what we have been acts negatively on what we can be. When I was a child I was a Christian; now I am one no longer. Does this mean, strictly speaking, that I do not go on being a Christian? The Christian I was, is he dead, annihilated? Of course not; of course I am still a Christian, but in the form of having been a Christian. Had I not known the experience of being a Christian, did I not have it behind me and go on being a Christian in this form of having been one, it is possible that, faced with the difficulties of life today, I might now resolve to be a Christian. And what has happened to me in this matter is happening to many Europeans, who *were* Christians either on their own account or vicariously, from the recollection of their forefathers. Who knows, if one got to the bottom of things, whether it might not be said that it is happening to everybody, including those who believe in all good faith that they still are Christians? That it is possible to be a Christian today, just like that, in the fullness of the term and without reservations, is not so very certain. And the same might be said about being "a democrat," being "a liberal," being *ancien régime*," being "feudal."

If I do not make love to Hermione, if I do not turn Christian, accordingly, if the reality of my life at the moment is what it is, what it is going to be depends on what is commonly called "experience of life." This is a knowledge of what we have been that memory has preserved for us and that lies always to hand, accumulated in our today, in our actuality or reality. And it happens that this knowledge determines my life negatively in its "real" aspect, in its being. And from this it follows that constitutively my life is experience of life. My fifty years signify an absolute reality, not because the body may be growing weak or the psyche losing its grip, things that do not always happen, but because at that age one has accumulated a longer living past, one has been more things, and one "has more experience." The conclusion to be drawn from which is that man's being is irreversible, he is compelled ontologically always to advance on himself, and this not because a given instant of time cannot recur: on the contrary, time does not recur because man cannot go back to being what he has been.

But experience of life is not made up solely of my past, of the experiences that I personally have had. It is built up also of the past of my forebears, handed down to me by the society I live in. Society consists primarily in a repertory of usages, intellectual, moral, political, technical, of play and pleasure. Now, in order that a form of life—an opinion, a line of conduct—may become a usage, a thing of social validity, it is necessary, first, that time should elapse, and second, that the form in question should cease to be a spontaneous form of personal life. Usage is tardy in taking shape. Every usage is old. Expressed differently, society is, primarily, the past and, relatively to man, tardigrade. For the rest, the establishing of a new usage—a new "public opinion" or "collective belief," a new morality, a new form of government, —the determination of *what* at each moment society *is going to be,* depends on what it has been, just as in the individual life. Western societies are finding in the present political crisis that they cannot, without more ado, be "liberal," "democratic," "monarchical," "feudal" or . . . "Pharaonic," precisely because they have already been these things, either in themselves or from experience of how others have been them. In the "political public opinion" of today, in the usage at present in force, an enormous amount of the past continues active; that opinion, that usage, is accordingly this past in the form of having been it.[14]

Let the reader simply take note of what happens to him when, faced with the great political problems of the day, he desires to take up an attitude. First there arises in his mind a certain form of government, let us say, authoritarianism. In it he sees, rightly, a means of surmounting some of the difficulties of the public situation. But if this solution is the first or one of the first to occur to him it is not by chance. It thrusts itself upon him precisely because it already lay there to his hand, because he did not need to invent it for himself. And it lay to his hand not merely as a project, but as an experiment already made. The reader knows, from personal experience or from reference, that there have been absolute monarchies, Caesarisms, unipersonal or collective dictatorships. And he knows further that all these forms of authoritarianism, if they solve some difficulties, leave others unsolved and in

---

[14] I have already shown excessive temerity, and incurred excessive risk, in thus attacking at the gallop, like the Median warriors of old, the most fearsome themes of general ontology. Now that I have come to a point where, if I were to be moderately clear, it would be necessary to establish carefully the difference between so-called "collective or social life" and personal life, I would ask permission to renounce emphatically any intention of so doing. Should the reader be moved to curiosity concerning my ideas on the matter or, in general, concerning the development of all that has preceded, he will find both set forth, as adequately as may be, in two books. In the first, under the title *El hombre y la gente*, I have tried faithfully to expound a sociology which does not, as in the past, avoid the truly basic problems. The second, *Sobre la razón viviente*, is an attempt at a *prima philosophia*.

fact bring new ones of their own. The reader is thus led
to reject this solution and to essay another in his mind
which will avoid the drawbacks of authoritarianism. But
here the same thing happens over again, and so it goes on
until he has exhausted all the obvious forms of government, those that lay already to his hand, those he knew
about because they had already been tried. At the end
of this intellectual journey through forms of government
he finds that, if he is to be sincere and act with full conviction, there is only one he could accept: to wit, a new
one, one different from any that has been before, one invented by himself. He must either invent a new being of
the state himself—even though it be only a *new* authoritarianism or a *new* liberalism—or search around for
someone who has invented such or who is capable of inventing it. Here, then, may be seen how in our present
political attitude, in our political being, there persists
all the past of mankind that is known to us. That past is
past not because it happened to others but because it
forms part of our present, of what we are in the form of
having been, because, in short, it is *our* past. Life as a
reality is absolute presence: we cannot say that *there is*
anything unless it be present, of this moment. If, then,
there is a past, it must be as something present, something active in us *now*. And, in effect, if we analyze what
we are now, if we take the consistency of our present and

hold it up against the light in order to reduce it to its component elements as the chemist or the physicist may an object, we find to our surprise that this life of ours that is always this, the life of this present, actual moment, is *composed* of what, personally or collectively, we have been. And if we speak of *being* in the traditional sense as a *being already* what one is, as a fixed, static, invariable, and given being, we shall have to say that the only element of being, of "nature," in man is what he has been. The past is man's moment of identity, his only element of the thing: nothing besides is inexorable and fatal. But, for the same reason, if man's only Eleatic being is what he has been, this means that his authentic being, what in effect he is—and not merely "has been"—is distinct from the past, and consists precisely and formally in "being what one has not been," in non-Eleatic being. And since we cannot hope ever to rid the term "being" of its traditional static signification, we should be well advised to dispense with it. Man *is* not, he "goes on being" this and that. The concept "to go on being" is, however, absurd: under promise of something logical it turns out in the end to be completely irrational. The term we can apply, without absurdity, to "going on being" is "living." Let us say, then, not that man *is*, but that he *lives*.

On the other hand, it is advisable to take due note of the strange mode of knowledge, of comprehension, repre-

sented by this analysis of what, concretely, our life, that
of the present, is. In order to understand my conduct with
regard to Hermione and to Christianity, or the reader's
with regard to public problems, in order to discover the
reason of our being or, what comes to the same thing, *why*
we are as we are, what have we done? What was it that
made us understand, *conceive,* our being? Simply the
telling, the narrating that *formerly* I was the lover of this
and that woman, that *formerly* I was a Christian, that the
reader in himself or through others he has heard of was
an absolutist, a Caesarist, a democrat, etc. In short, the
reasoning, the *reason,* that throws light here consists in a
narration. Alongside pure physico-mathematical reason
there is, then, a narrative reason. To comprehend anything human, be it personal or collective, one must tell
its history. This man, this nation does such a thing and is
in such a manner, *because* formerly he or it did that other
thing and was in such another manner. Life only takes on
a measure of transparency in the light of *historical reason.*

The most disparate forms of being *happen* to man. To
the despair of the intellectualist, *being* is in man mere
happening, happening to him: it "happens to him to be"
a Stoic, a Christian, a rationalist, a vitalist. It happens
to him to be the paleolithic female and the Marquise de
Pompadour, Jenghiz Khan and Stefan George, Pericles
and Charles Chaplin. Man does not actively subscribe to

any of these forms: he passes through them—he lives them—like Zeno's arrow, moving, in spite of Zeno, during the whole of its flight.

Man invents for himself a program of life, a static form of being, that gives a satisfactory answer to the difficulties posed for him by circumstance. He essays this form of life, attempts to realize this imaginary character he has resolved to be. He embarks on the essay full of illusions and prosecutes the experiment with thoroughness. This means that he comes to *believe* deeply that this character is his real being. But meanwhile the experience has made apparent the shortcomings and limitations of the said program of life. It does not solve all the difficulties, and it creates new ones of its own. When first seen it was full face, with the light shining upon it: hence the illusions, the enthusiasm, the delights believed in store. With the back view its inadequacy is straightway revealed. Man thinks out another program of life. But this second program is drawn up in the light, not only of circumstance, but also of the first. One aims at avoiding in the new project the drawbacks of the old. In the second, therefore, the first is still active; it is preserved in order to be avoided. Inexorably man shrinks from being what he was. On the second project of being, the second thorough experiment, there follows a third, forged in the light of the second and the first, and so on. Man "goes on being" and "unbeing"—living. He goes on accumulating being—the past; he goes on making for himself a being through his dialectical series of experiments. This is a dialectic not of logical but precisely of historical reason —the *Realdialektik* dreamt of somewhere in his papers by Dilthey, the writer to whom we owe more than to any-one else concerning the idea of life, and who is, to my mind, the most important thinker of the second half of the nineteenth century.

In what does this dialectic that will not tolerate the facile anticipations of logical dialectic consist? This is what we have to find out on the basis of facts. We must know what is this series, what are its stages, and of what nature is the link between one and the next. Such a dis-covery is what would be called history were history to make this its objective, were it, that is to say, to convert itself into historical reason.

Here, then, awaiting our study, lies man's authentic "being"—stretching the whole length of his past. Man is what has happened to him, what he has done. Other things might have happened to him or have been done by him, but what did in fact happen to him and was done by him, this constitutes a relentless trajectory of experiences that he carries on his back as the vagabond his bundle of all he possesses. Man is a substantial emigrant on a pilgrimage of being, and it is accordingly meaningless to set limits

to what he is capable of being. In this initial illimitable-
ness of possibilities that characterizes one who has no
nature there stands out only one fixed, pre-established,
and given line by which he may chart his course, only one
limit: the past. The experiments already made with life
narrow man's future. If we do not know what he is going
to be, we know what he is not going to be. Man lives in
view of the past.

*Man, in a word, has no nature; what he has is . . .
history.* Expressed differently: what nature is to things,
history, *res gestae,* is to man. Once again we become
aware of the possible application of theological concepts
to human reality. *Deus, cui hoc est natura quod fecerit
. . . ,* says St. Augustine.[15] Man, likewise, finds that he
has no nature other than what he has himself done.

It is comic in the extreme that "historicism" should be
condemned because it produces or corroborates in us the
consciousness that the human factor is changeable in its
every direction, that in it there is nothing concrete that is
stable. As if the stable being—the stone, for instance—
were preferable to the unstable! "Substantial" mutation
is the condition on which an entity as such can be progressive, the condition on which its being may consist in
progress. Now concerning man it must be said, not only
that his being is variable, but also that his being grows

---

15 *De Genesi ad litteram,* vi, 13. 24 (*Patrologia Latina,* vol. 34).

and, in this sense, that it progresses. The error of the old doctrine of progress lay in affirming *a priori* that man progresses towards the better. That is something that can only be determined *a posteriori* by concrete historical reason: it is precisely the great discovery we await from this, since to it we look for the clarifying of human reality and, along with this, for light on the nature of the good, the bad, the better, and the worse. But that our life does possess a simply progressive character, this we can affirm *a priori* with full evidence and with a surety very different from that which has led to the supposition of the improgressivity of nature, that is to say, the "invariability of its laws." [16] The same knowledge that discovers to us man's variation makes patent his progressive consistency. The European of today is not only different from what he was fifty years ago; his being now includes that of fifty years ago. The European of today finds himself without a living faith in science precisely *because* fifty years ago he did believe wholeheartedly in it. That faith that held sway half a century ago may now be defined with reasonable precision; were this done it would be seen that it was such *because* about 1800 the same faith in science wore a different profile, and so successively until we come to the year 1700 or thereabouts, at which date faith in reason is constituted as a "collective belief," as

[16] I refer the reader to the last words of note 13 on p. 207.

something socially operative. (Earlier than 1700 faith in reason is an individual belief or the belief of particular small groups that live submerged in societies where faith in God, if already more or less inert, yet continues operative.) In our present "crisis," in our present doubt concerning reason, we find then included the whole of that earlier life. We are, that is to say, all those forms of faith in reason, and we are in addition the doubt engendered by that faith. We are other than the man of 1700, and we are more.

There is no cause, therefore, for weeping overmuch concerning the mutability of everything human. This is precisely our ontological privilege. Progress is only possible to one who is not linked today to what he was yesterday, who is not caught for ever in that being which is already, but can migrate from it into another. But this is not enough: it is not sufficient that man should be able to free himself from what he is already and take on a new form, as the serpent sloughs its skin and is left with another. Progress demands that this new form should rise above the old and to this end should preserve it and turn it to account, that it should take off from the old, climbing on its shoulders as a high temperature mounts on lower ones. To progress is to accumulate being, to store up reality. This increase of being, it is true, when referred only to the individual, might be interpreted naturalistically as the mere development or *enodatio* of an initial disposition. With the evolutionary thesis still unproved, whatever its probability, it can be said that the tiger of today is neither more nor less a tiger than was that of a thousand years ago: it is being a tiger for the first time, it is always a first tiger. But the human individual is not putting on humanity for the first time. To begin with, he finds around him, in his "circumstance," other men and the society they give rise to. Hence his humanity, that which begins to develop in him, takes its point of departure from another, already developed, that has reached its culmination: in short, to his humanity he adds other humanities. He finds at birth a form of humanity, a mode of being a man, already forged, that he need not invent but may simply take over and set out from for his individual development. This does not begin for him—as for the tiger, which must always start again—at zero but at a positive quantity to which he adds his own growth. Man is not a first man, an eternal Adam: he is formally a second man, a third man, etc.

Mutable condition has thus its ontological virtue and grace, and invites one to recall Galileo's words: *I detrattori della corruttibilità meriterebber d'esser cangiati in statue.*

Let the reader reflect closely on his life, studying it

against the light as one looks at a glass of water to study its infusoria. If he asks himself why his life is thus and not otherwise, it will appear to him that not a few details had their origin in inscrutable chance. But he will find the broad lines of its reality perfectly comprehensible once he sees that he is thus because, in the last resort, the society—"collective man"—in which he lives is thus. And in its turn the mode of being of society will stand revealed, once there is discovered within it what that society was—what it believed, felt, preferred—at an earlier stage. That is to say that in his individual and fleeting today man will see, foreshortened, the whole of man's past still active and alive. For we can only throw light on yesterday by invoking the day before yesterday; and so with all yesterdays. History is a system, the system of human experiences linked in a single, inexorable chain. Hence nothing can be truly clear in history until everything is clear. We cannot properly understand what this "rationalist" European is unless we know exactly what it was to be a Christian, nor what it was to be a Christian unless we know what it was to be a Stoic: and so the process goes on. And this systematism of *res gestae* becomes reoperative and potent in history as *cognitio rerum gestarum*. Every historic term whatsoever, to have exactness, must be determined as a function of all history, neither more nor less than each concept in Hegel's *Logic* has value only in respect of the niche left for it by the others.[17]

[17] A simple example will make clearer what I have sought, with extreme concision, to convey in these last few lines. In an excellent book recently published by Paul Hazard, *La Crise de la conscience européenne, 1680–1715*, the third chapter begins thus: "*L'Europe semblait être achevée. Chacun de ses peuples avait des caractères si bien connus, et si décidément marqués, qu'il suffisait de prononcer son nom pour que surgît une série d'adjectifs qui lui appartenaient en propre, comme on dit que la neige est blanche et le soleil brûlant.*"

This means that about the year 1700 one of the active ingredients of human life here in the West was the conviction felt by European peoples that they knew one another. Let us admit the facts, referred to by the author, whose collective enunciation forms this proposition. Is this enough to make the proposition true? For it happens that exactly the same proposition might be valid for the life of Europe today. Who can doubt, nonetheless, that the knowledge of one another that European peoples believe they possess today is something very different from that of two centuries ago? And different, be it clearly understood, not solely nor chiefly by its content, but in the certainty, the fullness, the daily presence, and general sense it has for us. This means, however, that as an active factor in our lives its reality is in consequence very different from the reality of two centuries ago. Hence Hazard's proposition and the concept its terms express are inadequate, since they are equivocal. If they are valid for today, they are invalid for 1700. And if they are valid for both, they will be equally valid for 1500, for it is beyond question that then, too, the nations of Europe believed they knew one another. Now, in the measure in which a concept has validity for different epochs of humanity, it is an abstraction. Yet the conception that Hazard is trying to express is of an essentially concrete order, and it escapes through the abstract meshes of his proposition. Had this been thought in terms of the reality of 1500 and of that of 1900, for example, it is evident that it would have thrown much more light on what was in fact happening in 1700. In history there come in—and once it has resolutely constituted itself historical reason, there must come in still more—abstract concepts that are valid for whole ages and even for the whole of man's past. But this is a question of concepts whose object is also an abstract moment of reality, of the same degree of abstraction as themselves. In the measure of their abstractness they are clearly formal: they do not, in themselves, think anything real but demand to be made concrete. When therefore we say that they are valid for different ages, their validity is to be understood as one of forms requiring a content, as an instrumental validity; they do not describe "historic forces." An approximate analogy may be seen in geometrical concepts, which are valid for, but do not explain, physical phenomena, because they do not represent forces.

The need to think systematically in history has many corollaries, one of which is this, that it will have to increase substantially the number of its

History is the systematic science of that radical reality, my life. It is therefore a science of the present in the most rigorous and actual sense of the word. Were it not a science of the present, where should we find that past that is commonly assigned to it as theme? The opposite—and customary—interpretation is equivalent to making of the past an abstract, unreal something lying lifeless just where it happened in time, whereas the past is in truth the live, active force that sustains our today. There is no *actio in distans*. The past is not yonder, at the date when it happened, but here, in me. The past is I—by which I mean my life.

IX

Man stands in need of a new revelation. And whenever man feels himself in contact with a reality distinct from himself, there is always revelation. It does not matter what the reality be, provided it appear to us absolute reality and not a mere idea, presumption, or imagination of our own concerning a reality.

Physical reason was, in its day, a revelation. Astronomy previous to Kepler and Galileo was a mere play of ideas, and when one *believed* in any of the various systems then current or in such and such a modification of

terms and concepts. Naturalists will not take this amiss if they reflect that they possess today some millions of concepts and terms to describe the vegetable and animal species.

those systems, it was always a pseudo belief that was at issue. One believed in this theory or in that as a theory. Its contents was not reality but simply a "saving of appearances." Now the adhesion that a certain reasoning or combination of ideas commands in us does not go beyond these. Called forth by ideas as such, with them it ends. One believes that *within the sphere and play of ideas* these ideas are those best worked out, the strongest, the most subtle, but one does not on that account experience the devastating impression that in these ideas reality itself is breaking through, hence that they are not merely "ideas" but pores opening in us through which there penetrates into our consciousness something ultramental, something transcendent throbbing fearfully directly beneath our touch.

Ideas represent, then, two very distinct roles in human life. At times they are *mere ideas*. Man is aware that, in spite of the subtlety and even the exactitude and logical rigor of his thoughts, these are no more than inventions of his own, in the last instance an intrahuman, subjective, and nontranscendent activity. The idea in this case is the opposition of a revelation—it is an invention. But at other times the idea *qua* idea disappears, converted into a pure mode of sensitive presence elected by an absolute reality. The idea now appears to us neither as an idea nor as our own. The transcendent reveals itself to us on its own account, invades and inundates us—and this is the revelation.[18]

For over a century now we have been using the word "reason," giving to it a meaning that has become more and more degraded until today it signifies in effect the mere play of ideas. That is why faith appears as opposed to reason. We forget that at its birth in Greece, as at its rebirth in the sixteenth century, reason was not the play of ideas but a radical and tremendous conviction that in astronomic thought man was in indubitable contact with an absolute order of the cosmos, that through the medium of physical reason cosmic nature loosed within man its formidable and transcendent secret. Reason was, therefore, a faith. On this account, and on this account only—not in virtue of its other peculiar attributes and graces—it was able to wage war with the religious faith that till then had held the field. Vice versa, it has not been realized that religious faith is also reason, because of the narrow and fortuitous conception one held of reason. It was claimed that reason did not pass beyond what took place in laboratories or the cabalism of the mathematicians. The claim as we see it today is ridiculous enough—one form, it might be called, out of a thousand intellectual provincialisms. The truth

18 *Vide* the author's book, *Ideas y creencias*, Espasa Calpe, 1940.

is that the specific characteristic of religious faith rests on a structure every bit as conceptual as dialectics or physics. It is a matter of profound surprise to me that there should not yet exist—that I am aware of—any exposition of Christianity as a pure system of ideas, expounded as one may expound Platonism, Kantianism, or positivism. Did such exist—and it would not be a difficult task—its relationship to all other theories as such would become evident, and religion would no longer seem so abruptly separated from ideology.

All the definitions of reason that made its essence consist in certain particular modes of setting the intellect in operation have not only been narrow; they have sterilized reason by amputating or devitalizing its decisive dimension. To me reason, in the true and rigorous sense of the word, is every such act of the intellect as brings us into contact with reality, every act by means of which we come upon the transcendent. The rest is nothing but . . . intellect, a mere homely exercise leading nowhere, that first amuses, then depraves, and finally causes man to despair and to despise himself.[19]

---

[19] To Descartes, it must not be forgotten, truth is that specific characteristic of thought in virtue of which this transcends itself and reveals to us a being, brings us into contact with something that is not itself. The criterion by which we may distinguish when, in effect, thought does transcend is immanent in thought itself, this being the only means we possess of arriving at being. But the immanence of the criterion is not to be confused with that of the characteristic, "truth": the latter is not immanent, it is transcendence itself. "*La vérité étant une même chose avec l'être . . .*"

Hence the necessity in the present state of humanity to leave behind, as archaic fauna, the so-called "intellectuals" and to set our course anew towards the man of reason, of revelation.

Man has need of a new revelation. He loses himself in

Contemporary subjectivism is idealism. It maintains that there is no reality transcending thought, that the only reality or being is thought itself. A thing "has being" when we think of it as being—and hence that being is immanent in thought since it is very thinking. The consequence of this is to take away from the concept of reality as transcendence its primary, ingenuous, and sincere meaning. All reality is but thought reality, nothing more. On the other hand, it gives to everything thought a certain value as reality, as being, that it had not before. Before, the observation that something was only a thought implied that it had no reality whatever: it was *ens rationis*, the pseudo entity. Thus: the mathematician today holds a theorem true when he believes he has succeeded in demonstrating that the ideas composing it, as ideas and solely to the extent that they are ideas, fulfill certain requirements. That is to say, he considers his mathematics to be effective knowledge although it may have no validity—and he himself may have no interest in whether or not it has such validity—for any extraideal reality. He holds, that is, as truth a thought directed to an imaginary or intraideal being. Now the Greeks, the thinkers of the Middle Ages, and Descartes himself would call such mathematics poetry—since poetry is a thinking imaginary entities. They would not call it "knowledge." At the beginning of the century it was fashionable to forget this and to interpret Descartes arbitrarily, making of him an idealist. Descartes, it is true, prepares the way for idealism, but he is not yet an idealist himself. What gave rise to this erroneous interpretation is the fact that, purely because Descartes is not an idealist, purely because he does not suspect the idealist attitude, it never occurs to him to take precautions against such a failure to understand him. Be it recorded, then, that whenever Descartes speaks of "truth" and of "knowledge," he understands a thinking with the power to transcend itself, a thinking, that is to say, that poses a reality beyond thought, a reality outside itself. By mathematics he understands a science of realities, not of *entia rationis*, and by logic the same. It is for this reason that Descartes, like Leibnitz, who is already frankly half an idealist, cannot hold it sufficient to set out from a formal reality, that is, from one placed among ideas as such, but needs urgently a first truth in which formal truth, the truth set among ideas, shall be at the same time a real truth, valid for things, a truth, in a word, which will guarantee the transcendence of thought. Bordas-Demoulin was never more Cartesian than when he pointed out that the divine freedom, in creating truths and placing these in our spirit, appears to give to our knowledge the character of revelation. (*Vide* Hamelin, *Le Système de Descartes*, p. 233.)

the infinite arbitrariness of his inner cabalism when he cannot essay this and discipline it in the impact with something that smacks of authentic, relentless reality. Reality is man's only true pedagogue and ruler. Without its inexorable and sensitive presence culture, seriously speaking, does not exist, the state does not exist, even—and this is the most terrible of all—reality in his own personal life does not exist. When man is left, or believes himself left, alone with no reality other than his ideas to impose its stern limits on him, he loses the sensation of his own reality, he becomes to himself an imaginary, spectral, phantasmagoric entity. It is only under the formidable pressure of something transcendent that our person becomes compact and solid and we are enabled to discriminate between what, in effect, we are and what we merely imagine ourselves to be.

Now, physical reason by its very evolution, by its changes and vicissitudes, is come to a point where it recognizes itself as being mere intellect, if indeed as the highest form of this. Today we are beginning to see that physics is a mental combination and nothing more. Physicists themselves have discovered the merely symbolic, that is to say, domestic, immanent, intrahuman, character of their knowledge. In natural science these or those mutations may come about, Einstein's physics may give way to another, the quantum theory be followed by other theories, the electron conception of the structure of matter by other conceptions: no one looks for these modifications and advances ever to leap beyond their symbolic horizon. Physics brings us into contact with no transcendence. So-called nature, at least what the physicist examines under this name, turns out to be an apparatus of his own manufacture that he interposes between authentic reality and himself. And, correlatively, the physical world appears not as a reality but as a great machine ready to man's hand for him to manage and exploit. The faith that still attaches to physics today comes down to faith in the uses to which it can be put. What is real in it—and not mere idea—is only its utility.[20] That is why we have lost our fear of physics, and with fear our respect, and with respect our enthusiasm.

But whence, then, can there come to us this new revelation of which man stands in need?

Every disillusionment consequent on depriving man of faith in some reality on which he had set store brings into the foreground and permits the discovery of the reality of what remains to him, a reality that had previously escaped his attention. So the loss of faith in God leaves man alone with his nature, with what he has. Of this nature the intellect forms a part, and man, obliged to

[20] It is not extravagant to see a resemblance between what physics means to man today and what the *divinatio artificiosa* that Posidonius speaks of (*vide* Cicero, *De divinatione*, i) meant to the ancients.

have recourse to it, forges for himself his faith in physico-mathematical reason. Now, having lost his faith—in the manner here described—in that reason also, man finds himself compelled to take his stand on the only thing still left to him, his disillusioned life. And here we see why in our day we are beginning to discover the great reality of life as such, in which the intellect is no more than a simple function, and which possesses in consequence a more radical character of reality than all the worlds constructed by the intellect. We find ourselves, then, in a disposition that might be styled "Cartesianism of life" and not of *cogitatio*.

Man asks himself: what is this solitary thing that remains to me—my life, my disillusioned life? How has it come to being nothing but this? And the answer is the discovery of man's trajectory, of the dialectical series of his experiences, which, I repeat, though it might have been different, has been what it has been, and which must be known because it is . . . *the* transcendent reality. Man set outside himself is brought up against himself as reality, as history. And, for the first time, he sees himself forced to a concern with his past, not from curiosity nor in the search for examples which may serve as norms, but because it is all he *has*. Things are never done seriously until the lack of them has been seriously felt. For this reason the present hour is the appointed time for history to re-establish itself as historical reason.

Until now history has been the contrary of reason. In Greece the two terms "reason" and "history" were opposed. And it is in fact the case that scarcely anyone up till now has set himself to seek in history for its rational substance. At most, attempts have been made to impose on it a reason not its own, as when Hegel injected into history the formalism of his logic or Buckle his physiological and physical reason. My purpose is the exact reverse: to discover in history itself its original, autochthonous reason. Hence the expression "historical reason" must be understood in all the rigor of the term: not an extrahistorical reason which appears to be fulfilled in history but, literally, *a substantive reason constituted by what has happened to man,* the revelation of a reality transcending man's theories and which is himself, the self underlying his theories.

Until now what we have had of reason has not been historical and what we have had of history has not been rational.

Historical reason is, then, *ratio, logos,* a rigorous concept. It is desirable that there should not arise the slightest doubt about this. In opposing it to physico-mathematical reason there is no question of granting a license to irrationalism. On the contrary, historical reason is still more rational than physical reason, more rigorous, more exigent. Physical reason does not claim to understand what it is that it is talking about. It goes farther, and makes of this ascetic renunciation its formal method, the result being that the term "understanding" takes on a paradoxical sense against which Socrates already protested in the *Phaedo* when describing to us his intellectual education. The protest has been repeated by every subsequent philosopher down to the establishment of empirical rationalism at the end of the seventeenth century. We can understand in physics the analytical operation it performs in reducing complex facts to a repertory of simpler facts. But these elemental, basic facts of physics are unintelligible. Impact conveys exactly nothing to intellection. And this is inevitable since it is a fact. Historical reason, on the contrary, accepts nothing as a mere fact: it makes every fact fluid in the *fieri* whence it comes, it *sees* how the fact takes place. It does not believe it is throwing light on human phenomena by reducing them to a repertory of instincts and "faculties"—which would, in effect, be crude facts comparable to impact and attraction. Instead it shows what man does with these instincts and faculties and even expounds to us how these facts—the instincts and faculties—have come about: they are, of course,

nothing more than ideas—interpretations—that man has
manufactured at a given juncture of his life.

In 1844 Auguste Comte wrote: *"On peut assurer au-
jourd'hui que la doctrine qui aura suffisamment expliqué
l'ensemble du passé obtiendra inévitablement, par suite
de cette seule épreuve, la présidence mentale de l'avenir."*
(*Discours sur l'esprit positif*, ed. Schleicher, p. 63.)

Afterword by John William Miller
The Ahistoric and the Historic

I THE AHISTORIC

WE NEED NOT take too seriously the current objections to metaphysics. Anyone who looks farther than his nose may find himself wondering what lies over the horizon. No one takes satisfaction in the narrowness of his outlook nor could he appear to do so without a disguised pretentiousness like that of Antisthenes the Cynic, to whom Socrates commented that his pride showed through the holes of his ostentatious rags. We like to inhabit a world, and indeed are sure to do so if we enjoy so much as a local habitation and a name. The first personal singular pronoun is no denotation word corresponding to some object of consciousness: it is rather a reflective word, a mark of self-consciousness and therefore of an equally ideal environment in terms

237

of which the self articulates its identity. The traditional distinction between appearance and reality is no more than the attempt to establish the personal pronoun, to make it articulate, and, at the same time, to avoid the victimization which threatens any extension of the immediate into its environment. In all pretentions to finitude there lurk the conditions which allow it to be identified. We are told from early years that infinity is a mystery and that we do not understand it nor can hope to do so. But no infinity is any less a mystery than the finitude of which it is the condition and the meaning. Apart from that no infinity could be suggested.

The motive of the many endeavors in making and characterizing this distinction between appearance and reality has not been intellectual, but voluntaristic. Immediacies seemed unorganized and therefore a threat to the powers of the self and to the clarity of objects. It is not only an ideal object that metaphysics has been charged with proposing, but also an equally ideal subject. There was no secure antecedent self and then a casual interest in an environing world; the question has been, rather, how to establish the self by providing the sort of world in which it could function. In "The Sentiment of Rationality" William James proposed that no acceptable philosophy could disqualify our cognitive and moral powers. He would have as our world only that situation which warrants and fulfills our own energies. In this abstract form his proposal was not novel, but for the sake of meeting this basic demand he did not shrink from proposing a pluralistic universe, aware as he was of the oddity of such an adjective.

Metaphysics, then, is no attempt to evade immediacies. It aims rather to get them established. This aim has never been undertaken in cold blood, but always with an intensity and ardor which to many has seemed not the least count in the indictment. Yet one may expect something more than prosaic sobriety when a man tells what he is or what he is up to. A man is not disturbed in his world if he is not disturbed in himself.

The mistrust which philosophy has frequently encountered appears on the surface to be the consequence of extravagant conclusions; but its deeper source lies in the dislike, or even the dread, of maintaining the actuality of limitation. For that is self-consciousness and reflects its urgencies and responsibilities. A search for reality has also been a search for the self. And where the self is not actualized in that search, it has not yet put in its appearance. When, however, through adopting the thought of others a reality appears ready-made, the self becomes conventional, irresponsible, and dogmatic. That the world be ready-made has even seemed at times a philosophic propriety. Its typical form is real-

ism. The reaction to realism is scepticism. The sceptic
sees no continuity between himself and the ready-made
world. Then appearance asserts itself as no less absolute than reality but lost in its isolation and impotence.
Idealism occurs as a reaction to both realism and scepticism; and its characteristic quality is found in a re-
version to an ancient definition of the world as the perfection of an ordered finitude. In all these instances,
appearances draw their status, their authority or lack
of it, from a reality which exceeds finitude. When that
environment has been viewed as absolute it has become
ahistoric, including time or casting it off as illusion,
but in either case denying it a constitutional status.

Historicism is the affirmation of the constitutional in-
terdependence of center and environment; this relation
includes all the efforts which have been made to define
it. It is the view that historical time, *i.e.*, dated time, is
constitutional and not derivative from any antecedent
account of a timeless situation. Obviously this can be
the only basis for a philosophy which proposes to include history as a category. Let history be derivative,
let it be irrelevant to the maintenance of the distinction
between appearance and reality, and one deprives it
of ontological force. If thought has taken flight into very
remote regions it has done so in order to illuminate the
closer immediacies which, unenvironed, present neither

a world nor any coherent finitude. Then we have conjured up visions more vast than dreams and much more persistent. For now as in the past we call that our world which gives status and authority to the immediate. The record of these endeavors is history. There the modes of self-definition become explicit and serve as the vehicles for an understanding of what we have become.

Among the ideas which extend and organize immediacy, none has been more current than that of "nature." Nature is an idea, not a fact. It is not somewhere or somewhen, it has no latent heat, specific gravity, or co-efficient of expansion. It is an answer to the need of understanding immediacies. It is no hypothesis explaining particulars in one way rather than in another. It is the objectivity which establishes the subject, the reality which explains appearance, the constancy which orders variety. These were the considerations which accompanied its discovery and which marked the endeavor to render immediacies intelligible.

And so, when Ortega says in a key sentence that "man has no nature, what he has is a history," it is plain that he is making a statement about the organization of immediacies. Whether or not there is a historical way of extending experience is the problem of a philosophy of history. Insofar as anyone would endorse that way, he would do so for the reason that not all immediacies find extension in nature. Why would they not? It is because nature seems not defined in terms of a past, whereas man is not defined without it. This past is not the uniformity of anonymous change where all our yesterdays have been as today. History presents a past which the present does not illustrate—indeed, the past may be darkly mysterious—so that only after many years and much soul-searching can one come to understand the forces which generated Amiens, and the Parthenon, the *Divine Comedy* and *The Clouds*.

Man, thinks Ortega, is what he has become and, what is more, what he has made himself to be by his own reflective thoughtfulness. Nature is a constitutional sameness, history is a constitutional revision of all systematic identity. We stand in history only as our tomorrows will not be as today, when, indeed, our yesterdays will seem puzzling and unintelligible. Sometimes we get mildly scolded by interested parties because we have lost touch with the twelfth or thirteenth centuries or with colonial America when that "fierce spirit of liberty" of which Edmund Burke spoke was taking shape. But a historical past arises from neglect, and has to be discovered anew. That is a mark of its historical status. So long as the classical world had not been rediscovered, after having been lost and superseded, neither its wonders nor its limitations could be deliberately known and appreciated.[1] The flavor of the past is lost without the sauce of the present. There is no past except as it has been obscured and its influence re-established. One type of ahistoric mind laments the present which needs to rediscover its heritage. It would prefer a present which had never felt its distinctive novelty nor suffered any estrangement from its progenitors, wishing men other than they have come to be and invoking criteria of excellence which stand aloof from time and its transforming energies. The Autocrat of the Breakfast Table, who lived in Boston but made visits to Parnassus, observes archly, "There was Aristoteles, a very distinguished writer of whom you have heard—a philosopher in short, whom it took centuries to learn, centuries to unlearn, and is now going to take a generation to learn all over again." The forces once operating and now forgotten or underestimated establish their authority only when the present requires them for the understanding of its own constitutional confusions and for the composure of its resolves.

The American Civil War marked a "new birth of freedom"; and in the tight argument of the Cooper Union speech, Lincoln, who knew that we could not escape history, set out the genealogy of the attitude toward slavery. The denial of political equality had turned out to be

[1] See E. Panofsky "Meaning in the Visual Arts" especially ch. 1 and 5.

worse than had been supposed and its assertion much better. But these were the disclosures of time. As well look for gravity where no object moves in space as for historical forces which are to be discerned before their presence, and so their power, gets reaffirmed in their consequences. History is no job for the reporter who thinks he owns the categories of description. The historian is your true contemporary. He stands in new conditions, and must do so, if the old are to exhibit vitality and relevance. He represents genealogical novelty. In philosophy nothing can be more deadly than what so often passes for its history. One cannot look for history apart from the urgency of its present interpreter who knows that the past has been its own critic and therefore entails for its understanding a novel, but derived and responsible, sequel—a perilous endeavor indeed. Not the least distinction of Kant occurs in his calling David Hume "that great man," although he disagreed with him and amended him. The past derives its life from the original vitality of its heirs.

As an idea, history will seem no more clear to us than the idea of nature. Its force will not be felt except as a reaction to the powerful authority of the impersonal regularity and immutable constancy of the objective world. It was nature which established the subject as a category of experience. We have, therefore, a great stake in it, nothing less than the identification of the personal consciousness. It is an error, then, to see in nature nothing but the enemy of the self. Nature is its complement. Scratch the scientist and discover the devotee. Nature appeared as the great emancipator not because it saved us from illusions, but because it made possible their identification. In order to do this, the idea of nature had to establish, not abolish, the subject as the locus of illusion. In this aspect of nature occurs the reason for its remarkable tenacity as an idea. It brings us to ourselves.

The idea of nature is not confined to any particular account of what it may be that stands apart from subjectivity. Early philosophers saw the impersonal in many ways. There were the four or five "elements," atoms, numbers, the Platonic "ideas," the four causes of Aristotle, and there were also the good and the beautiful. The ahistoric has taken many forms. It seems fair to say that Ortega is not denying that man has a "nature" in order to reject materialism. What he is rejecting is the orthodox and persistent view that to understand is to invoke the immutable. This appears to be the core and center of his statement that man has no nature. What he does not want is an account of experience which omits time and self-revision as fundamental controls.

If time is not a constitutional factor of experience, it

is threatened with disappearance in that Truth, or in that Reality, which is without yesterdays. This view of the nature of things Ortega calls "Eleatic," from the city in southern Italy where there appeared a number of men who argued, with originality and brilliance, that change, and thus time, was an illusion and not reality. To Elea there came about 540 B. C. the philosopher Xenophanes, whose native city was Colophon in Asia Minor. He was a monotheist and he rejected the current anthropomorphic view of the gods, much as we might deny that truth and reality are measured by finitude. "But mortals suppose that the gods are born (as they themselves are) and that they wear men's clothing and have human voice and body." Anticipating Plato, he says further, "Homer and Hesiod attributed to the gods all things which are disreputable and worthy of blame when done by men." A second and more celebrated figure was Parmenides. He says of the One Being, "It is unmoved, in the hold of great chains, without beginning or end, since generation and destruction have completely disappeared and true belief has rejected them. It lies in the same, abiding in the same state, and by itself . . . but it is lacking in nothing." Plato, an admirer of Parmenides, also spoke favorably of the sort of knowledge that is "fastened as by a chain," and he searched for what remained the same—the colorless, odorless, unchanging essences, the patterns fixed in heaven. The third Eleatic, Zeno, is perhaps the best known. It was he who contended that Achilles the swift-footed, the goddess-born, could not really overtake the slow-coach tortoise once that plodding reptile had, with incautious hubris, been allowed a start in a foot race. It stood to reason, argued Zeno, that one could not additively exhaust the infinite. And since the real is the intelligible, motion which entails infinity even in its briefest extent could be no more than the illusion of appearances. Henri Bergson and Bertrand Russell have not thought it anachronistic to have a go at this annoying problem, although for different reasons and with different results. Russell retains the Eleatic proclivity to put reason in charge, whereas Bergson sees in motion an intuitive immediacy associated with vitalism and with action.

Reason unified. So it was believed. A perfect rationality would then propose a unity in which all change was absorbed into an imperturbable constancy. This unity has been called substance, Being, process, law, and much else. No literate man in the Western world, nor even an illiterate, lacks acquaintance with this way of making sense out of change. We have inclined, on the whole, to the view that it was the proper way. Reason has led us into some Eleatic Absolute, mundane or celestial, to some reality where time and finitude are absorbed, where they lack authority and become subordinate and derivative, the manifestations of another power, and so without original jurisdiction of their own.

Philosophy began as the cult of the rational. There is a story about Thales of Miletus which says that when he had at last brought a problem in geometry to a solution he went to the altar of his house and made grateful sacrifice to the god. Why should he not indeed? This was no longer Miletus, it was a world, and he the individual whose pure thought shared in the general order of spatial form which prevailed also in Ephesus and Sardis. The universal was the medium which sustained both the objective order of appearance and the thoughtful self-control of the individual. Even into modern times the philosopher has suggested the person who has thought for himself in systematic ways. Some colleges still have chairs of "natural philosophy"; and at the beginning of the nineteenth century laboratories were equipped with "philosophical instruments." Nature is not another object upon which we expend a bit of attention to the imprudent neglect of household chores or to the damage of higher purposes. Nature is the articulate objectification of finitude in its impersonal mode. The infinite is the form of finitude; and, conversely, the finite is the actuality of the infinite. Form is not fact, but function.

Order, and the absoluteness which it entails, has always seemed incomprehensible to the passive; while to the intense, nothing has seemed more evident than the close association of formal functioning with the reality of the self, and, on the other side, with the reality of nature or the supernatural. There is no sort of access to any Eleatic being apart from a process which is itself the antithesis of an immovable result. Confusion and darkness did not come into experience as data passively perceived or intellectually devised. They have rather been spoken of as features of a restless selfhood, inseparable from an endeavor to organize the immediate. The *Confessions* of Augustine, like Platonic dialogues which are also confessions, exhibits a search for both selfhood and order, no more for one than for the other. Eleaticism in all its forms is an egoism which has discovered the subjective without recognizing that the ideal is nothing alien, but rather the formal condition if its own identification. When, once in Miletus, Thales sacrificed to the god, it was no common man who was moved to do so, no formalist indeed, no doctrinaire, but rather a person to whom form had become his personal actuality.

The alliance of the individual and the universal may be observed in grave personal difficulties and conflicts.

A man with a universal is likely to allow it to become demonic and fanatical.[2] He will be all for unity and dead set against variety, for cause and against purpose, for the individual and against the state, for virtue and against cakes and ale. If the universal shows us a world there may be deformity and fanaticism in it. And yet what would you? Where the self is not defined in commitments, it has no actuality. It cannot be even wicked. In Kipling's poem, Tomlinson is turned back from the portals of both heaven and hell. Dante finds in the inferno one who had made the great rejection, *"il gran rifiuto."* And the apocalyptic writer declares, "I know thy works, that thou art neither cold nor hot: I would thou wert cold or hot."

Ortega sees in natural science a chief modern vehicle of the ahistoric temper. In it, too, changes are summarized in a uniformity which spreads over yesterday and tomorrow. There one deals with the impersonal and anonymous, with the repeatable. It is often held that "prediction" alone bears the mark and stamp of knowledge. There an expectation according to rule is verified by the event. This belief is part of a powerful climate of opinion. The event is in time, but the rule is not in time, conveys no date, and holds no less in Poonah than

[2] See Paul Tillich, *The Interpretation of History*, Part II (Scribners, 1936).

in Pisa. Prediction is the evidence that a constancy has been formulated and that as things have been they remain. There may be no final formula, but that is not the point. The point is, rather, that when we shall have come to know better it will be in terms of a more exact and inclusive rule. Only in that way are we saved from the darkness of a discrete multiplicity.

The same order which dispels confusion is also believed to save us from impotence. Power is the sign of a congruence between the act which is local and a state of affairs on which it can draw for desired results. A favorable outcome testifies that one's act has been addressed to responsive forces. Owen Glendower could call spirits from the vasty deep. The priests of Jehovah knew how to summon a consuming fire. Now one steps on the gas and rolls a mile a minute. Yet the exercise of this sort of power leaves the operator in a condition of insecurity. Whether incantations or gas engines will "work" is not, alas, a foregone conclusion in all specific circumstances. One awaits authentication. A hypothesis must be "verified" or confirmed. Prediction stands, then, as the dependence of a subjective state upon a region which is not included in the subjective consciousness. One may wonder to what extent the current search for security may be a consequence of the systematic separation of the subjective from an objectivity to which it must incessantly appeal for confirmation. Knowledge-seeking can become a sort of status-seeking. The very knowledge which, as Bacon observed, brings power, lacks autonomy and solicits an alien approval. Such knowledge and such power are precarious. In a paradoxical statement Bacon observes that "nature to be commanded must be obeyed." Command suggests authority, obedience submission. When, as in the scientific treatment of man, the alleged commander becomes himself the object of knowledge, his authority is dissolved in the implied extension of objective regularity to his own behavior. Not even the subjective then retains any systematic rôle in the description of knowledge. Thereupon knowledge vanishes, as the tension which sustains it slackens into passivity.

The ahistoric ideal has not however prevented the return of persons to the theater of inquiry. Eminent scientists aspire to be "original" and "creative," as if the discovery of formulas expressed no formula, as if there were untrammeled forces out of which a vast and encompassing regularity could emerge. The poet, "his eye in a fine frenzy rolling," has claimed no more. A trust in the personal operator also appears in the proposal that we "reduce the degree of empiricism." [3] This is a view of the scientist's work which puts more emphasis on

[3] J. B. Conant, *Modern Science and Modern Man* (Doubleday, 1953).

"policy" than on the disorderly rout of empirical sense
data. (The idea of sense data is not empirical, but let
it pass.) If, however we are to crossexamine nature, not
to say ourselves, we must feel empowered to ask questions. A question is a formality—how many, how large,
how often, with what relation to other experiences? And,
of course, any question entails the assumption that the
way of finding an answer is not altogether unknown.
Only a good deal of study puts one in the way of asking
the sort of question which opens up an area of sustained
investigation and discloses the distinctive factors which
control a specific discourse. It is confidence in this basis
of inquiry which reduces the degree of empiricism, fo-
cusing attention and excluding those sensations and per-
ceptions which, as psychology, have as much right as any
other, and thus legislates with increasing precision the
relevance of observation itself. As science has grown
more "pure," more in control of quite conceptual entities and relations, less defined or not at all defined in
terms of the objects of purpose and of common sense, it
has transferred the order of objective nature to the order
of the questions which allow a systematic inquiry. It
seems plain that there are no questions and no cross-
examinations without formalities.

This more or less deliberate transfer of the locus of
order from what is observed to the authoritative ques-

tion of the inquirer and observer is a characteristic mark of the difference between the outlook which had developed from Descartes and that which had prevailed up to the seventeenth century. It would be a mistake not to see in this a shift in the direction of the historical. In the categories of any area of knowledge we now tend to see our own work; and this the more unquestioningly because our most general and basic concepts of order have been revised, and because these revisions have dates. Nevertheless, one has not moved from Eleaticism into history because of a transfer of anonymous uniformity from the absolute object to the equally dateless formality of a question. But the fact that it is now the question which conveys the stable and the constant does, however, put one in a position to ask about the genesis of these trusted guides. The order of that genesis is history. The chief figure after Descartes who put the form of questions in a nonempirical position was, of course Kant. It was he who allowed us, and even constrained us, to construe the "nature" of physics as an organization of experience according to rule. In the history of philosophy Kant's formalism is the monumental arrest of the anarchy of Hume. Because of the categories, radical empiricism was "reduced." After Kant, the story moved with slow and halting pace toward the genesis of the categories themselves; and of this deep change

Hegel is the principal author. Kant had left the phe-
nomenal world of nature quite ahistoric. It was as anonymous as you please and dealt only with consciousness
in principle, with *Bewusstsein überhaupt.*

The Eleatic unity, impersonal, dateless, anonymous,
has thus served to permit, not to block, the advent of history. It is great fun to see the past as a wretched mistake,
and to plume oneself on one's emancipation from its
darkness. But then all one's novelties are miraculous.
The bankruptcy of the past offers poor security for the
solvency of the present. Nor does it seem likely that a
dull and nerveless ancestry will beget genius in its descendants. There is no radical revision without an
equally powerful fixity. History is the revision of out-
looks, not of opinions. It is not the correction of factual
errors within a static control. It is a modification of the
mode of making errors. The truth does not make us
free; what frees us is the control of the form of truth.
And that is not logic or mathematics, but history. But
history could not appear until truth itself, in its fixed
anonymity, in its vastness and grandeur, became itself
the prison of the spirit. The Eleatic, the ahistoric, is a
historical necessity. The status of the categories must be
nonaccidental if they are not to relinquish legislative
authority; but it must also be derivative if they are not
to remain arbitrary. History is the absolute empiricism

which generates the categories of truth. But that is a longer story than can be here suitably attempted.

II THE HISTORIC

The ahistoric has enjoyed much prestige, particularly for the reason that it gave status to the thoughtful individual. It seemed the region of our freedom because it carried beyond appearance and accident to the supremacy of order and so of our intelligence. There we shared the way of the world and rescued ourselves from unstable opinions and shifting desires. These adventures had their emotional side and aroused deep feeling. The need was urgent, the result often imposing. Like all aspects of self-consciousness, nature grew from tensions, from unquiet, from intensities of concentration. All the great ahistoric formulations still make this demand when we try to understand them. Nor is there any other way. Whether we seek acquaintance with the Stoics or with the powerful fervor of Augustine, we have to tune ourselves up to the hazards they faced, and to the results which appeared to them composing and validating. Emotion is not altogether psychological, aroused by accident, and so passing away with casual adaptations or with equally casual changes in the environment. There are emotions of actuality, the existential tensions of persons.

Emotion is the mark of intimacy, of promise or menace. We are not moved where nothing of ourselves is at stake, nor enduringly moved apart from some mode of attaining and preserving our functioning actuality. But there is another intimacy, that of time and deeds. The self-consciousness of early man had a temporal as well as a timeless aspect. In *The Ancient City*, Fustel de Coulanges presents an admirable account of early classical identity. Its keynote is piety, as Aeneas was "pious"—looking after his father and carrying his lares and penates to Latium. The person stood in his family. He had known ancestors and a household altar where he kept burning an undying flame. The slave and the uprooted stranger lacked these requisites of full personal status. These lesser beings were not involved in the continuity of time. They owned no burying ground for their dead, performed no rites, lacked the obligations of descendants and the anticipations of regard and service from their posterity.[4] Identity derived from the actual life of a particular family or tribe, and later from citizenship in a polis. Like the household, the polis, too, had its shrine and its rites. In declining an opportunity to escape from prison and prospective death, Socrates, as late as 399 B. C., voiced an ancient sentiment. For he

[4] See the early chapters of Walter Pater's *Marius the Epicurean* for a similar story.

was the son of Sophroniscus, an Athenean, and Athens herself was his civic mother. He could not see himself wandering about in Thrace without home and so without recognition. Ostracism was no small penalty then, nor is it today; although its basis has changed. The person in full force, exercising his functions, securing respect and recognition, could be found only in a temporal continuum. It is misleading to suppose that there was an objective time in which some men were persons, others not. The activities which made the time peculiar were those of the men who could act; they made the time. To be recognized as acting is to be accepted as sharing in the existence of a place and time. Objects are taken into account, or not, as one may feel disposed, but persons are there only because they cannot be ignored. Such individuals were, of course, caught up in strong feelings. Much was at stake, themselves indeed. Some may consider these early modes of identity "superstitious," but one may venture to say that superstition is only what comes to be regarded as an inadequate mode of personal identification. When, as in some modern philosophies, identification becomes in principle superstitious, nature, along with the self, vanishes in a general crash of existential order.

Identity takes time. No person, no nation, no outlook exists in the present tense alone. In his notable but neglected *The Problem of Christianity,* Josiah Royce speaks of "Time and Guilt" and of "Community and the Time Process." A community exists in its career, in the recognition of its self-maintaining piety. A society needs to be reaffirmed—sometimes through the vicarious atonement made by those not guilty of a specific crime, avowing through their own sacrifice the absoluteness of the values which a crime has threatened. But the individual, too, needs time for the discovery of his deeper controls. Nobody can know what he has to do until his impulses disturb, or even nullify, the institutional conditions of their satisfaction.[5] We are not in charge of ourselves except as we take into account what we have done. The moving finger writes our fate only if what has been written gets appropriated and becomes a source of identification. There is no other fate than this. Nature is no fate except in the history of its formulations. But this fate is the same as our finite and temporal actuality. There we maintain ourselves in those infinities which are also the sole evidence of our self-possessed finitude.

Where there is no documented history we fall back on myth. We devise a past which gives character and direction to the present. Hesiod wrote of the "Five Ages," the times that were gold, silver, bronze, the age of demi-

---

[5] See W. E. Hocking's excellent *Human Nature and its Remaking* (Yale, 1918).

gods, and now the time of iron—which he deplores. An underived present robs one of an attitude toward the concrete immediacy. In the *Statesman* Plato traces present discontents to the decline that set in after the age of Cronus. This is the other side of his attempt, in the *Timaeus,* to give the state a cosmic authority. We look before and after and pine for the continuum of our present actuality. When we discover that the past is other than we took it to be, our present confidence is disturbed. Is it really possible, the student may ask himself, that Plato showed some doubt over the ability of the "idea" theory to satisfy the motives which launched it? Is there scant evidence for the story that George Washington cut down his father's cherry tree with his little hatchet and could not tell a lie about it, while there is good evidence that he did excoriate a delinquent officer in language hardly appropriate to the Father of his Country? If anyone doubts his alliance with time, let him consider the reluctance, or even the dismay, with which he receives modifications of history. It can be very upsetting, and many have found it so. And, of course, history books offer a splendid opportunity for the censor. The myth makers are not all of them ancient. A principal reason for scientific history derives from its power to protect our identities. Personal existence is not anonymous nor are deeds facts of nature. They are in-

dividual and call for that unique continuum which ex-
tends a present—not the dateless present—into its distinctive past. He who can confuse a past brings ambig-
uity into the present and erodes its will. To control a
past, as in a dogmatic declaration of what took place,
is also to control a present. Ardors and intensities ac-
company the discovery of the individual no less than
those which glow in the great formulations of the ahistoric.

Nature is our first explicit morality because there we
are all together and no one must fabricate nor proclaim.
On the whole, we have by now worked into the clear
on this point. History is the second morality, and its
force is but vaguely felt. Individuality and history are
fateful modes of the actual; and we get some idea of
their current feebleness when we consider the great success of the psychological view of man as wanting to be
"adjusted" to his environment. This is the erosion of intensity, the substitution of conformity for personality
and of success for passion. We try to circumvent fate
and call it truth. We debase great men when we see them
as servants of our desires rather than as the architects
and the summoners of our self-hood.

To a larger extent than we are aware we live through
the past tense. The modes of this continuum are obvious
enough, but they lack accredited status. We need a new

epistemology, one that does not shrink from giving on-tological status to artifacts. The past rides on them, and they are symbols and voices. We know quite well that we use words and that without expression in its various forms, without ritual and ceremony, nothing of the past would be available. A large dictionary tells what a word "means" by supplying an account of the past usages which mark its career. A word means what it has come to mean. A misused word is no factual error, but an assault on one's functioning, as when the "uninterested" man is said to be "disinterested." The outlook disclosed in such abuse can halt a conversation and raise doubts about the suitability of a political candidate. And it cer-tainly should. Your egghead is a man who can speak without abusing the language. To a lawyer the law is what it has become. The specification of actual cases when a rule has been applied and qualified, far from detracting from the force of law, adds to its weight and authority. A rule without antecedents, without liability to revision, lacks, in the end, any relevance to meaning. No articulate control can flout the medium in which it is expressed. One can not have one's words and eat them too. Yet this is what all ahistoric views of man propose to do. There is no saying of words, as against the making of noises, apart from what has been said. He who wishes to speak must learn a language. Nor is this a practical matter between two or more persons who, apart from words, share a common world and need only put convenient labels on objects or on acts independently known. All expression is a discipline, and it is time that we abandon the nonsense of supposing ourselves antecedently in possession of a world of which linguistic is only a handy memorandum—as if we knew about Hamlet apart from the play, or about freedom apart from the institutions which have emerged as its vehicles, about physics apart from actual yardsticks, and about man apart from his history.

Of course there are some persons who would prefer Hamlet without the King of Denmark, the murderer king, not an inspiring example to the nation's youth. Among philosophers many deplore the errors of the past. It could not be said of David Hume that he endeavored to save the world for God, but he did try to keep it from going to the devil. He became, in a manner of speaking, a book-burner, saying of any work which seemed to him unreliable, "Commit it then to the flames. For it can contain nothing but sophistry and illusion." One can sense the exultation with which logical positivists tell us that there is nothing to lose but our chains when we rid ourselves of words which have no "literal significance." [6] In fact, the words which they reject do

[6] See, for example, A. J. Ayer, *Language, Truth and Logic* (Dover).

have a "literal" significance and only that; and that is why they are the vehicles of ideas, and not marks on paper or tickets of admission to sense data. They are the literate words. From the point of view of the history of philosophy one cannot escape David Hume, nor would one dream of committing him to the flame of purification. To see the point of that inevitability is to stand in history. There one is hospitable, never censorious from a point of view which alleges independence of time. Emerson observed, "There is one mind common to all individual men." The price of the one mind is the individuality of one's own.

A rule purporting to be independent of history, aloof from occasions, operates only as a blind natural force. It can be objected to only by force. The trouble with crime, as with dogma, is that it generates no precedents. It is the lawyers who have the precedents. But the violators of the law are no more arbitrary than are the judges when the latter use words exempt from the controls of time.

Such considerations may seem homely and familiar, and one might wish for heavier themes such as "causation" in history, the effectiveness of the hero, or the influence of the transcendent. Yet, if history is to be universal, one needs to feel its presence before talking much about it. So we need to see it around us and in the substance

of our experience. Every distinctive finality is the articulation of an immediacy, not as content, but as form
and so as an energy. That the form of finitude is always an infinity, and articulate, is the central theme of
a philosophy of history. This is the anti-Eleatic factor
of experience. Obviously, any "theory" of history is a
mistake, as is also any "theory" of knowledge. Such
procedures foreclose the possibility of making time a
category. It is to history, not to theory, that we must go
if the actual is to shine by its own light and not be obscured in the light which is also the total darkness. Philosophers have been concerned with saving the appearances; if history be a philosophical idea it can only propose to save the moment. This is very hard to do. Ideals
are fairly easy to come by and they may even seem
reasonable. But a child can scatter them in the fasci-
nated glow of some trivial absorption, thereby bringing
humiliating qualms to the observer. The fugitive mind
evades the conditions of the lucid moment. It shrinks
from the implications of intensity. No doubt it is very
difficult to let the moment declare its authority. As a
general thing we prefer to regard the moment as subordinate, seeing it from some position which is never
itself actual. And certainly, except as the moment operates as the point of departure of formal order, one
cannot avoid trying to control it from an Eleatic posi-

tion. But that is a self-deception, and it ends in conflicts and frustrations. It is hard to be in history. It is harder to make history. As a rule we prefer to be right.

It is usually said that Herodotus is the father of history. Toynbee translates his reasons for writing: "Herodotus of Halicarnassus presents the results of his researches in the following work, with the twofold object of saving the past of mankind from oblivion and ensuring that the extraordinary achievements of the Hellenic and the Oriental worlds shall enjoy their just renown—particularly the transactions which brought them into conflict with one another." Of the glorious action at Thermopylae Herodotus says, "The Lacedaemonians fought in a way worthy of being recorded"; and again of Marathon, that the Atheneans "fought in a manner worthy of being recorded." Here was an interest in the past now valued for its own sake. The human spirit, its craft and courage, its weakness and power, were declared memorable and so rescued from an oblivion which would not only obscure a just fame but impoverish the heritage, dim the identity, and dull the energy of every self-conscious person—whether Greek or Barbarian.

Nor does Herodotus narrate the story of the conflict in a moralistic temper, the upright on one side, the miraculously wicked on the other, virtue and truth leading the assault upon miscreants and idolators. Herodotus saw the Persian wars as a development of long-standing differences which had originated centuries ago as incidents of egoism and of trade. He was dealing with the acts of men; and he looked upon them as fascinating revelations, as the naturalists had noted the planets and the stars, the seasons and the weather. The past became relevant to the comprehension of the present. This too is a piety.

Who, then, is in history? Anyone whose life has shape and who exerts himself to preserve his integrity has joined articulate forces. This need not be on a grand scale. It can mean no more than doing one's job and keeping the home fires burning. A great deal of our work is no better than maintenance. Most schooling is of that sort, and most teaching. We have a rendezvous with our time and place, and that is as much of destiny as is generally possible. Once in a blue moon one may hear an original word. Such a word is a disciplined qualification of a past. When it happens we mark a date, a moment stands out, a revelation has been made, a present glows, not with a hard gemlike flame, but with the warmth of an assured actuality. It is these actualities which, for their apprehension, impose a task. They can be grasped only as one takes the trouble to appropriate the mode of order in which they have been expressed. "Every oracle must be interpreted by the same spirit which gave it forth."

The past is forever at the peril of time. It has to be maintained. But no man can be forced, or cajoled or argued into history. The future, when there is one, is the fatality of the historical present, and this is no matter of fact, but a matter of will. Plainly, this is no place to look for bland placidity. All that history has to offer is our actuality. It cannot be administered. It takes nerve, or, as Ortega suggests, it is a sporting proposition.

At the outset it was suggested that objections to metaphysics are to be entertained with reserve. The universal in all its forms loses its nonhumanity when contemplated through the motives which operated to produce it, rather than through its relation to any possible specific experience or purpose. The universal lies in the line of action and of function. But Eleaticism, in its anxiety to compose appearances, overlooked the controls of its own endeavors, namely the establishment and the maintenance of the immediate. In consequence, the immediate was lost *sub specie aeternitatis*. It was sought apart from time, apart from a past, where no finitude could generate a future as the fatality of its self-conscious present. The very intensity which produced it, those arresting and distinguished concentrations upon the factors of the actual moment, were lost sight of in the devouring result. But, of course, it took time to see that. The Eleatics did not know that they were Eleatics.

Historicism does not propose an alternative answer, a better one, a truer one. It notes the difficulty of setting out on a journey when the point of departure lacks articulate definition and when horizons are detached from any point of view. One cannot go somewhere from nowhere, especially if no person is there to take a step. The immediate comes into historical position when it stands in its career. Time comes of age through its own passage. Eleaticism is an imposing and a moving monument; but as a finality it is the denial of the energies which so gallantly sought some significance in the moment.

Williamstown, Mass.
October 6, 1960

Selections from the Norton Library